Use Scribus

THOMAS ECCLESTONE

NONFICTION BOOKS BY AUTHOR

APPLICATION GUIDES
Celestia 1.6 Beginners Guide
Use Opera: The Internet Browser

DOCUMENT PRODUCTION
Use Magix Photo Designer: A Beginners Guide
Use Scribus: The Desk Top Publishing Program

OFFICE PRODUCTIVITY
Use LibreOffice Writer: A Beginners Guide
Use LibreOffice Impress: A Beginners Guide
Use LibreOffice Base: A Beginners Guide
Use LibreOffice Calc: A Beginners Guide

COMPANY MANAGEMENT SOFTWARE
Use Podio: To Manage A Small Company

CONTENTS

DEDICATION

This book is dedicated to my mother for all her help.

1 FIRST STEPS

Scribus is a free open source Desk Top Publishing program that you can use to produce beautiful printed documents such as brochure, booklets, and letter heads for company stationary. It has all the same functionality as some of the major commercial DTP software and it's pretty easy to use as well.

This chapter will take you through the process of installing the software, and a first initial tutorial that will show you the first stages of the program.

By the end of this chapter you'll be able to produce a basic document in Scribus.

Installing GhostScript

GhostScript is a program that allows Scribus to do a PostScript Print Preview, and which also provides many useful fonts. While I suggest (recommend!) that you install it before you install Scribus it's not technically necessary to do so. Scribus will work without GhostScript but not necessarily quite as well!

You can find out information about how to install GhostScript for all operating systems at http://wiki.scribus.net/canvas/Ghostscript

In this book I'll take you through installing it in a 64 bit windows operating system. The steps are very similar for most operating systems although they can vary a little as explained in the above link.

The first step is to go to the location of the GhostScript download via the browser...

You'll see a list of download choices. Both for a commercial version and a GPL version. Click on the version that you want to download.

Platform / License	GNU Affero General Public License	Artifex Commercial License
Ghostscript 9.15 for Windows (32 bit)	Ghostscript GPL Release	Ghostscript Commercial License
Ghostscript 9.15 for Windows (64 bit)	Ghostscript GPL Release	Ghostscript Commercial License
Ghostscript 9.15 for Linux x86 (32 bit)	Ghostscript GPL Release	Ghostscript Commercial License
Ghostscript 9.15 for Linux x86 (64 bit)	Ghostscript GPL Release	Ghostscript Commercial License

In this case I started the 64 bit version for windows. The browser will start to download.

Click on the box when it's finished to run the application, or open the download folder and double click on the program that you downloaded.

You'll have to click Yes to the dialogue asking if you want to allow the program to make changes to the hard drive.

Read the License Agreement and click  if you do.

There's a dialogue saying how much space you have to install, and giving you a destination folder.

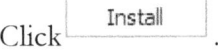

I think that it's generally very important to keep this folder the same because if you change it Scribus may not be able to find the new installation location and won't automatically detect the program. This could cause some hassle trying to alter Scribus so it detects the correct location.

Click 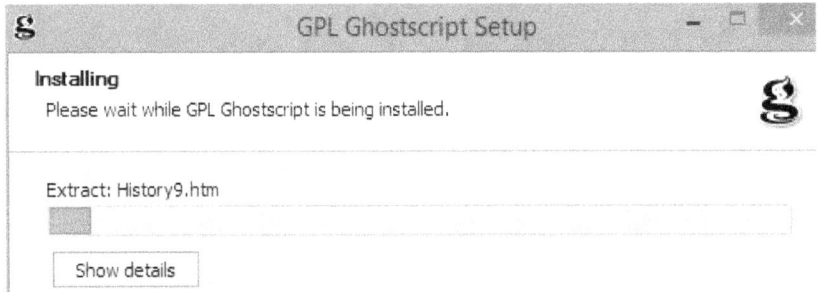 .

You'll see a progress bar. This may take some time.

When you finish you'll get a message that informs you the installation is complete. I suggest

leaving selected. But

I'd click the tick next to because it's really not that

useful when you're just using GhostScript with Scribus.

Then click [Finish] . You'll briefly see a command window appear as GhostScript installer carries out its final tasks, and then the computer will return to normal.

Now you've installed GhostScript (or chosen not to) you can install Scribus.

Downloading and running the Scribus installer

First google Scribus download

You'll see a download link from Scribus.net. Click on the link.

Scribus
www.**scribus**.net/ ▾
Scribus is an Open Source program that brings professional page layout to Linux, BSD UNIX, Solaris, OpenIndiana, GNU/Hurd, Mac ... **Download scribus**.png.
Download - Scribus Documentation - Scribus Wiki - About

The download page will display a list of stable versions. While it's possible to download a version of the software that is in development these versions can have errors or other problems. So it's generally better to download a version that is described as stable because they have been fully tested.

Click on the version that you want from the list:

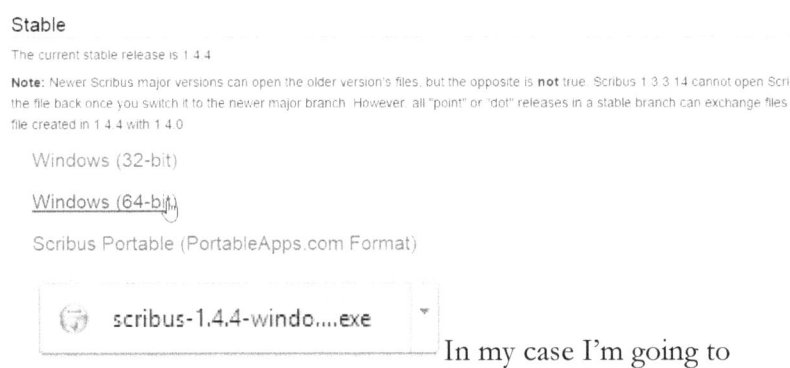

In my case I'm going to choose the Windows 64 bit version because of the operating system that I am using. There are a lot of operating systems that are supported. Although this book focuses on Windows, you will find that although other versions look a little different in general the same principals about how to use the program apply.

When you click on the link you'll be taken to a site called sourceforge. Don't worry about this. Sourceforge is a very common software repository for open source software.

Depending on your operating system when the page loads the download should start immediately. It's a big file so it's worth going and making a cup of coffee while it loads. In chrome you'll see the download icon at the bottom of the screen. (Other browsers vary)

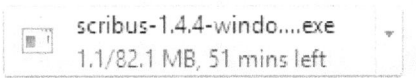

When the download is finished open it. For example by clicking on the box in Chrome.

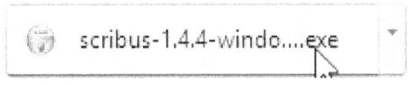

And hitting open. Alternatively, you can go to the downloads folder and double click on the file that you've downloaded:

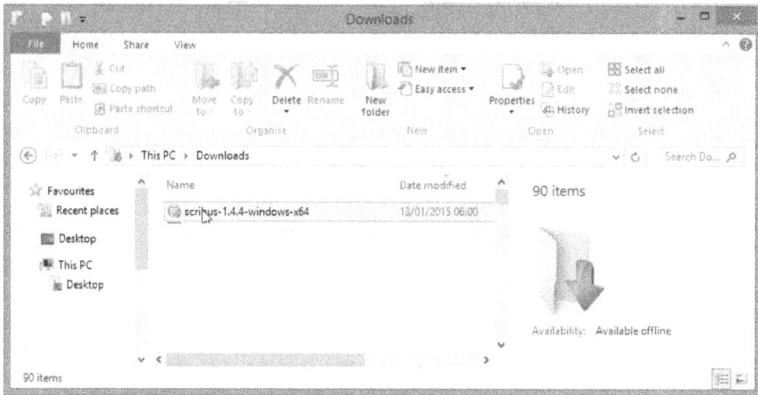

Windows shouldn't give you a smart scan warning when you run the file; it does, scan the file with your antivirus software and make sure that it is safe to use. Sometimes when downloading files they become corrupted. That's the most likely cause of the error and if that's the case you'll have to download the file again.

When you run the file you'll be asked if you want to allow it to make changes to the hard drive. Click on Yes.

The Installer will prepare to run.

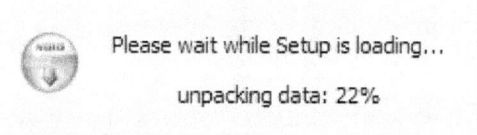

The first screen will ask you to select a language. The default is normally English. If you want another language click the box that contains the language name and choose it.

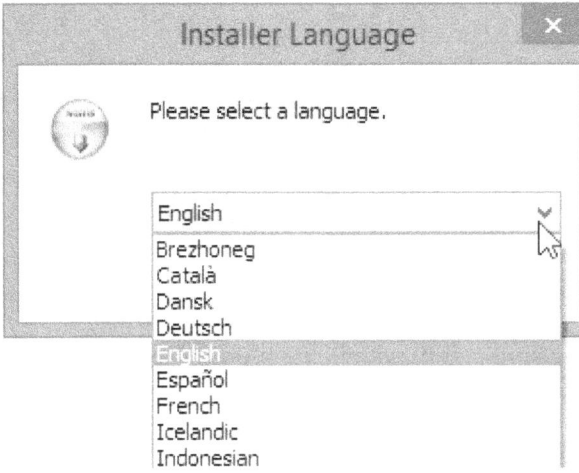

When you're happy that you have the correct language click OK .

You'll see a message asking you to close down all the applications. Close them down and then click Next > .

Read the license agreement. If you're happy with it, click the round circle next to I accept the terms of the License Agreement and then click Next > .

The next screen allows you to choose what components to install. I recommend keeping the default Full installation option. This allows you to access all the functionality of the program.

You can choose to remove components from the installation. For example, Additional Fonts or the desktop shortcut. As a rule I think it's best to keep all of these options, but sometimes you may not need any extra fonts or won't want Scribus to be available to all users.

☑ Scribus Files (required)
☑ Additional fonts
☑ Desktop Shortcut
☑ Shortcuts for All Users

When you're happy click ⬚ Next > .

The next screen will tell you how much space you have available and where you are installing at present.

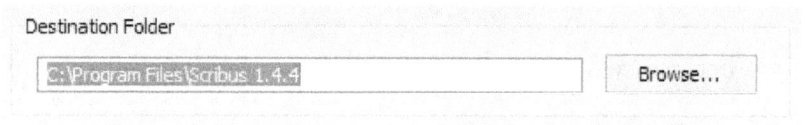

The two main times you'll want to change directory is when you're running out of space on the current drive (for example, because you've got an account with limited privileges on a network) or where you are running more than one installation at once. You can change the destination by clicking on ⬚ Browse... which will open a browse for dialogue. You can go through the directory list to find your current location

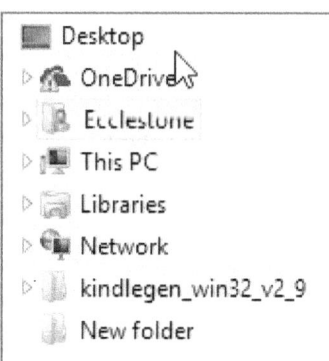

Clicking on a directory with a ▷ to expand it (i.e. show any subdirectories). When you've selected your route directory you can

click on 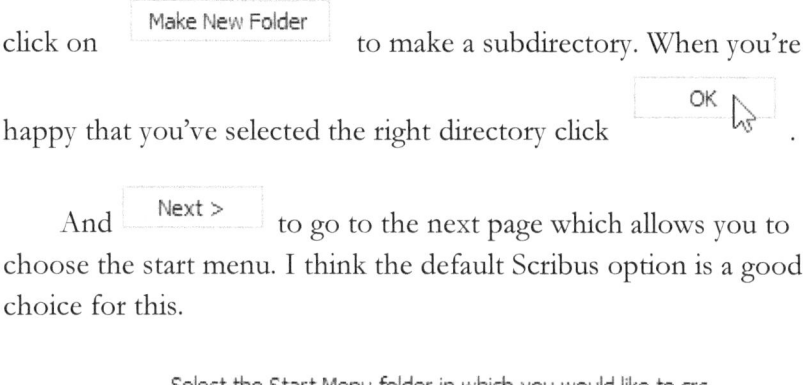 to make a subdirectory. When you're

happy that you've selected the right directory click 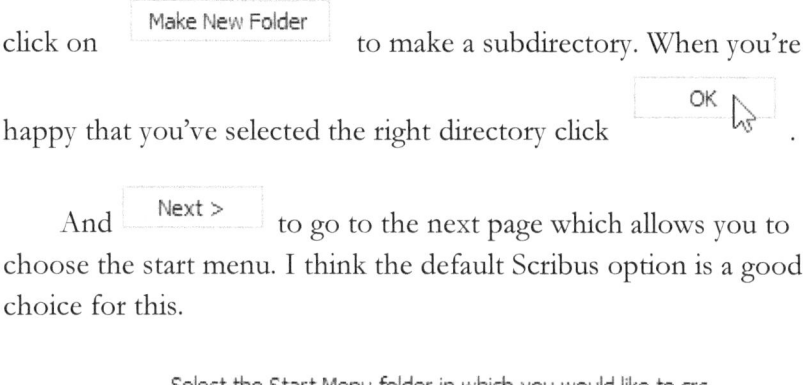 .

And 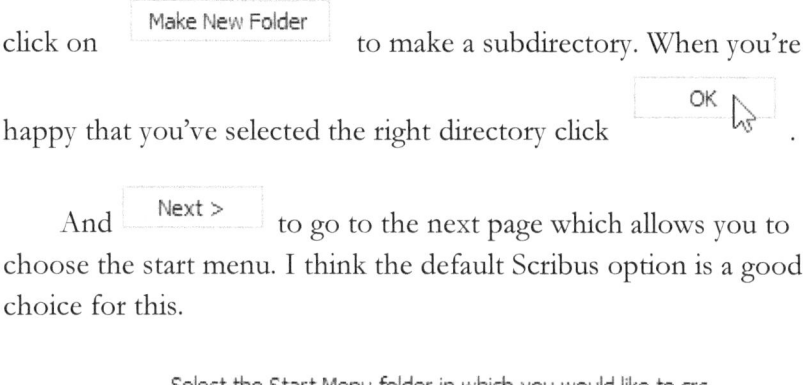 to go to the next page which allows you to choose the start menu. I think the default Scribus option is a good choice for this.

Select the Start Menu folder in which you would like to cre can also enter a name to create a new folder.

Scribus 1.4.4

But of course you could rename it by typing a name into the box, or you could double click on one of the existing groups:

Accessibility
Accessories
Administrative Tools
Adobe
AMD Catalyst Control Center
Communication and Chat
Comodo
Embedded Lockdown Manager

If you want to use a category that you've already created.

Once you've made your choice you can still change your mind

by clicking < Back but when you click Install the installer will start to install the program.

You'll see a progress window. Might be worth going and making a nice cup of tea or coffee since it sometimes takes a little while to carry out this step.

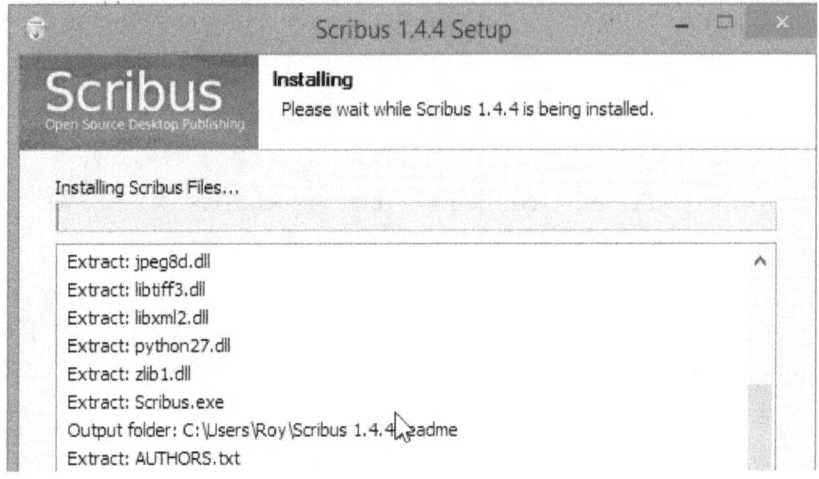

But when it's finished, you'll see a message dialogue with

Completing the Scribus 1.4.4 Setup Wizard

Which means that the installation has been successful.

Leave the tick ☑Run Scribus 1.4.4 selected if you want to run the program right away. If you leave ☑Show Readme selected it'll show you a read me with information about the program. The first time you install Scribus you may want to read this file but you'll often click on the ☑ to deselect this option.

When you've decided what will happen after you close the installer press [Finish] .

If you decided to run the installer after installation you'll see a Scribus splash screen start. The Program is beginning to run. The first time any user runs Scribus it can take a lot longer to run than normal. It's doing a lot of work behind the scenes. Normally it will run much more quickly.

Note that if you chose not to install GhostScript at an early stage in the installation when Scribus opens you'll see a message:

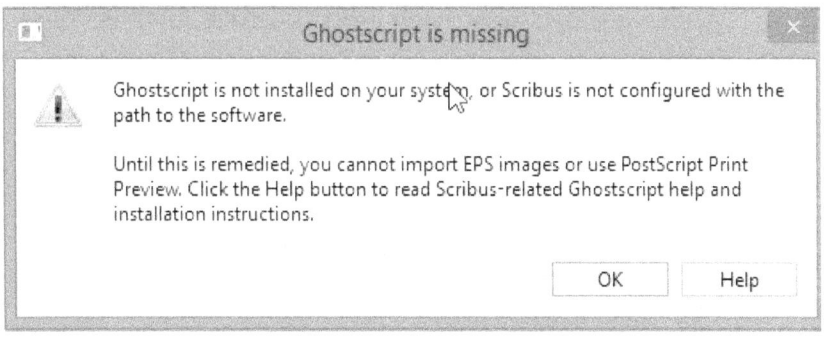

You can press OK to dismiss the message.

2 CREATING A DOCUMENT

This tutorial will take you through the first steps in Scribus. After completing this tutorial you should be able to do many of the most basic things that you'd expect from a desk top publishing program.

Page Layout

The first screen you'll see when Scribus opens up is the New Document Screen. In this tutorial I'm going to make a very simple Single Page document. A basic letter head. So, make sure that Single Page is selected:

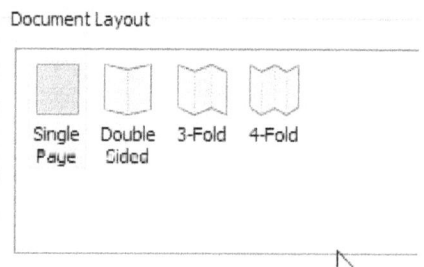

On the right of the document layout is a size option. The default is A4 in the UK, but may vary in other countries such as the United States. Click on the down arrow to select from the list of standard sizes.

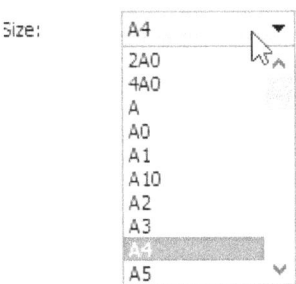

I'm going to stick with A4 in this example, although you may want to change it to whatever format your project demands.

The next option, Orientation, controls which way the paper is supposed to be.

Choose the Orientation that you want. I've chosen Portrait since this is a standard business letter.

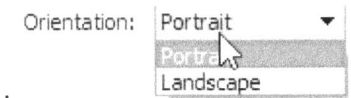

You could choose not to use a standard paper format, and instead use a custom paper format if you've got special paper in your printer.

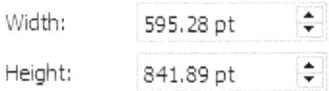

What is pt? Points is a typesetting measurement. Most font sizes are in points. But that's often not helpful for people that are new to desk top publishing. You can choose to use a measurement that makes more sense by clicking on the default measurement

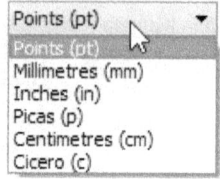

And selecting something that makes more sense, such as

Default Unit: Millimetres (mm) ▼ or inches.

You can also and edit the Number of Pages: [1] if you're doing a multipage document. You'll find that if you need to add or remove pages later on it's easy.

Margins

You can think of margins as the edge around your document. For example the top edge is the top margin:

Scribus provides some default margins which you can edit in this dialogue.

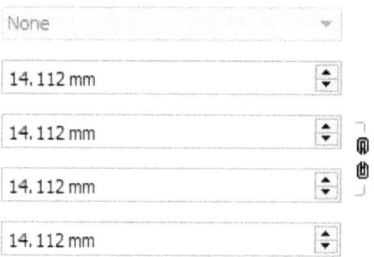

Note that sometimes you may choose not to use Margins. For example if you're creating a cover page, or a menu. Most text heavy documents like letters and books have relatively large margins. This not only looks neater but allows people to turn pages without having to dirty a page, and puts the text away from any centre crease.

Scribus also allows you to set bleeds. This is an area which is left blank to allow for printing area for books and other printed documents. Without a bleed subtle variations in where the book is cut would result in unpleasant looking documents.

Click on the ⟨Bleeds⟩ tab to change the page bleeds.

Automatic Text Frames

Scribus can generate Text Frames automatically for you. A Text Frame is an area on a document where you can type text. As a general rule I think that it's best to add text frames yourself.

New From Template

While we're not using it in this example Scribus does come with a number of templates that you can use for standard tasks. Click on the ⟨New from Template⟩ tab to see template examples for things like magazines.

You can also click on the ⟨Open Existing Document⟩ tab to open an existing document, or the ⟨Open Recent Document⟩ to open a document that you've been editing recently

When you're happy

When you're sure that you have all the settings set up the way you want them click on ⟨OK⟩. Remember that while it's possible to change most of these settings latter on if you want to it can get difficult once you populate a document with frames, images and other features. So double check that you've got everything set up the way that you want it.

Once you click on OK your document will be created and you'll be able to add new features.

3 TEXT FOR YOUR NEW DOCUMENT

In this part of the tutorial we're going to actually start making documents.

But first... Scribus is a Desk Top Publishing program. This means that you're working on a Document which can be anything from a single sheet of paper to a hundred page book. But a Document with no content is pretty much useless.

The content that you add to the document are called Objects. And the most common of these Objects are called Frames. For example you can add a Text Frame which is an area of text in the document. Or an Image Frame which is an image. And you can put frames on top of each other, allowing you (for example) to put Text on top of an Image in a cover.

Because you're always able to move objects around the page, or change which objects are on top of other objects, you gain a fine control over the appearance of a document.

In the last step we created a document. This step is to add content to it.

Getting to know Scribus

When you open Scribus for the first time you'll see quite a

complex looing window. Some of it you'll be familiar with if you use a word processor like Word or LibreOffice. Other parts of the screen will look less familiar.

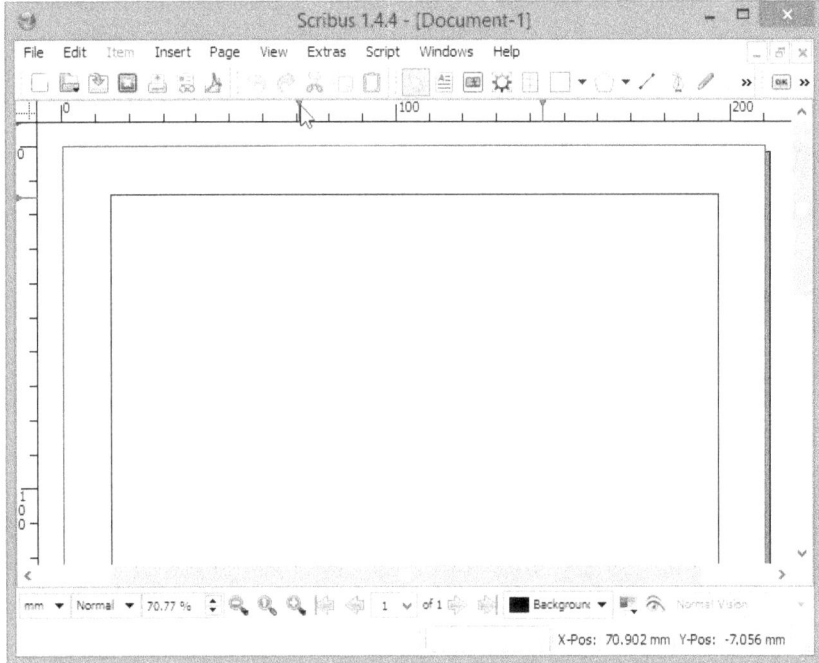

The centre of the page, surrounded by a red outline, is the main Document View. This allows you to see the content of the current page of the document.

At the top of the screen is the title which consists of the version number of Scribus and the document name.

Scribus 1.4.4 - [Document-1]

Under this is a menu bar. Lots of users will be familiar with this feature. It allows you quick access to a range of common tasks, for example opening files or adding pages.

File   Edit   Item   Insert   Page   View   Extras   Script   Windows   Help

Then there is a toolbar.

Next are Rulers. These are interesting features. They provide an indication of where you are in the page. There is a ruler at the top of the screen and to the left.

There are two red lines that move as you are moving the mouse. These indicate where on the document you are. You will often find that they make it easier to place items precisely.

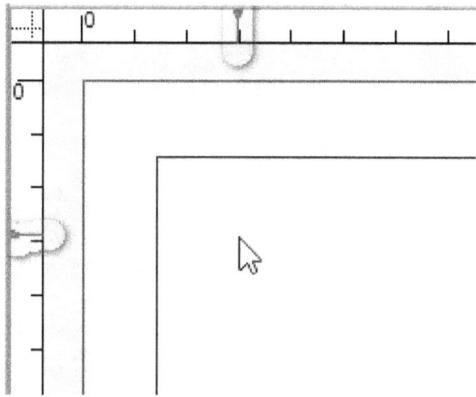

You'll also notice that below the Document is another toolbar. This toolbar can vary depending on what you're currently working on, but at the moment it should display document options. For example, you can use it to control the zoom and what page of the document you're editing.

Adding a Text Frame

We've just covered a lot of details. But since we've just got a blank document at the moment the most obvious first step is to put some text into the document. We can do this by adding a text frame.

You can do this by clicking 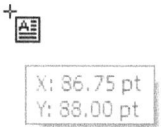 in the Insert menu. Alternatively, when you don't have any frame or object selected just type the letter T. You'll see the mouse pointer change:

Go to the position in the document that you want the frame to begin (for example the top right hand side). Click and hold the mouse button, then move the mouse to the opposite corner (i.e. the bottom left hand side of the text frame):

Notice above that while you're drawing it you can see a tooltip (the text near the mouse) of how wide and high it is. You can also see the box highlighted in blue. When you let go of the mouse you'll see that the frame has been drawn on the document:

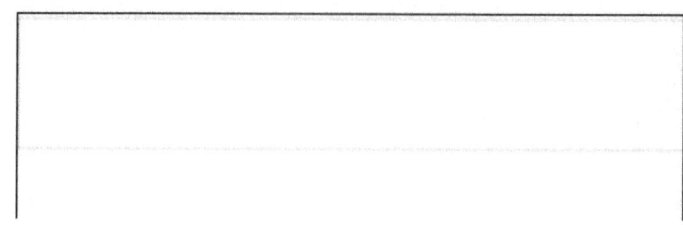

It looks like an empty blue box. So, that's the first frame that you've drawn using Scribus. For the moment you've got a problem. An empty Text Frame isn't much use. There are two ways to type text into the frame. You can both move the mouse over the frame and double click, which will give you a text prompt (note the flashing line) and simply type text.

You can enter text directly|

This is quick but you can't control the Font or appearance of the text very easily.

To control the appearance of the text you can use the second method. Right click on the text frame, then select Edit Text... Ctrl+T . This will open the Story Editor.

Story Editor

Often when using a piece of software like LibreOffice or Microsoft Word you'll edit in a completely WYSIWYG (What You See Is What You Get) fashion. But Scribus isn't completely a WYSIWYG editor. It can take a little time to get used to some of the quirks.

The Story Editor is divided into a menu bar, a toolbar with a lot of font options

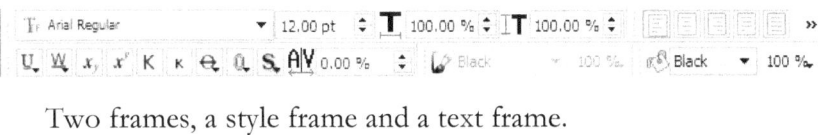

Two frames, a style frame and a text frame.

Plus some useful statistics.

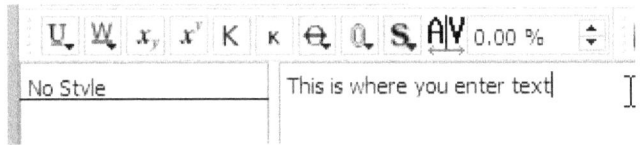

The first thing to do is enter some text. We click on the frame on the right hand. This displays a prompt. Then we can type in some text.

When you're typing in text you'll see that each paragraph has a style. That's on the Left hand side. The paragraph that you've selected has been given the default value of no style.

Let's change the Display Font first.

Changing the Display Font

The display font is one that's used in the Story Editor to display text. It isn't the font that you'll see in the document window. Click on 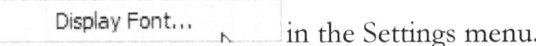 in the Settings menu.

You'll see a Font Window. The current name of the Font, Font Style and Size will be listed at the top.

Font	Font style	Size
Times New Roman	Normal	8

You probably don't have the same font choice as I've got above. This depends on the default display font that you've got on your system. I find it difficult to work with a font that's so small. So I'm going to scroll down in the Size list, and choose a font that's larger such as 12 point:

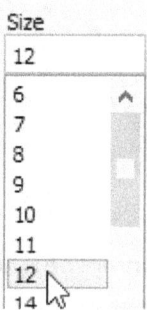

When you click on an option from one of the lists you'll see that the preview font changes:

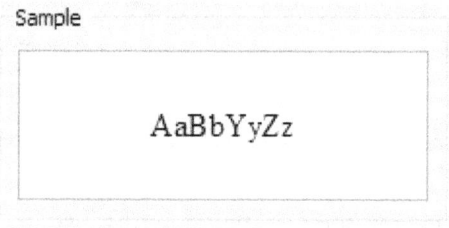

You can also change the Writing System to a non-default method of writing such as Greek, Hebrew etc. Obviously this book is based on the English language and doesn't go into how to use Scribus in a foreign language setting with much detail. But it is possible.

When you're happy with your font selections click on . You'll see the Font in the Story Editor Change:

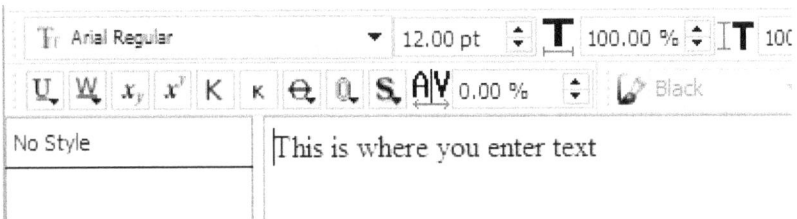

What you won't change is the actual appearance of the text in the document. To do this you need to use a slightly different approach.

Changing the Actual Font of Text in the Editor.

It would be boring if every document – or even every part of a document – had the same text. While it's important not to go overboard and go all "Fontitus" it's also nice to have different fonts for words that you might want to emphasis, for headers and other purposes.

You can change Font in two ways. Using styles, which I'll discuss later, or using spot changes. In many ways it's better to use a standard styles approach. This allows you to update the appearance of every paragraph or character with the appropriate style in one move.

However, for the moment we're going to make spot changes in style. In other words we will change the style only of a particular part of the document that we're editing. To do this, select the text whose font you want to change:

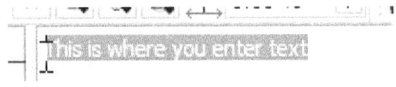

Remember the Font Toolbar?

We can use the option on the Toolbar to change the font. Some of these options are fairly obvious. For example, if we click on the

Font Name box 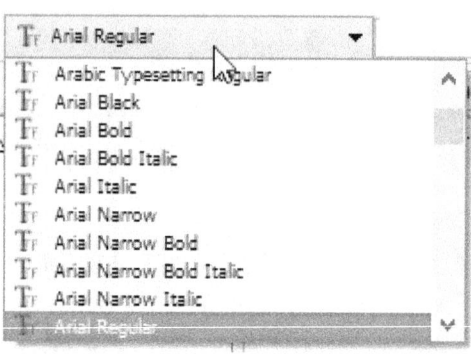 Scribus will then display a list of fonts for you to choose from. Scroll down until you find the font that you want to use.

I selected 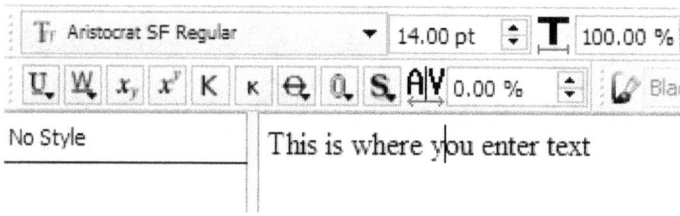 . Then I changed the font size to a slightly larger font: 14.00 pt. But hang on! Something odd's happened! If we look at the Story Editor window we'll see..

Nothing's changed in the Editor box!

Don't panic. As I said, the Story Editor isn't WYSIWYG. And one of the consequences of this is that you don't necessarily get a preview of the font that you're going to use when you're editing the text.

There's another little quibble that you'll notice. Once you've changed the Font, click at the end of the text and enter some more:

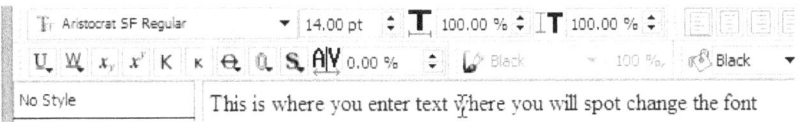

It looks like the text that you've just added is still the same font that you chose before. But if you highlight the text which you've added you'll find out the truth:

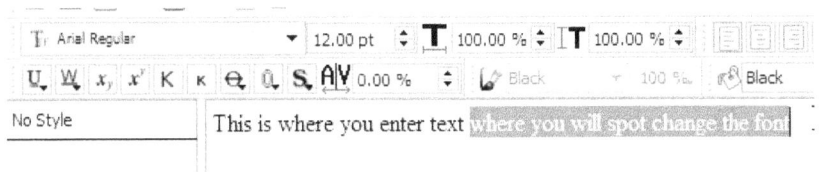

This is something to be very careful of when editing text using spot changes. It's almost always better not to edit text until it's all been added to the Text Frame. Then it's best to edit fonts in one pass only using spot changes very conservatively.

We'll go into a lot more detail about these options later.

Loading Text from a File.

Because Scribus is a Desktop Publishing program rather than a word processor it's often the case that instead of editing text directly in the Story Editor you'll use some other program to write the document and then import the text.

Personally that's how I deal with large documents. I think that there are a lot of which are much easier to work with than Scribus when you're actually **writing** large amounts of text. Out of all the word processors you can use with Scribus the free software package LibreOffice is excellent (I might be biased because I wrote a beginner's guide to using that called Use LibreOffice Text Writer).

One of the real advantages I find to using LibreOffice with Scribus is that importing formatting works better than when trying to import text from Word even if you save the word document in ODT (open office) format.

For example, take the following LibreOffice document:

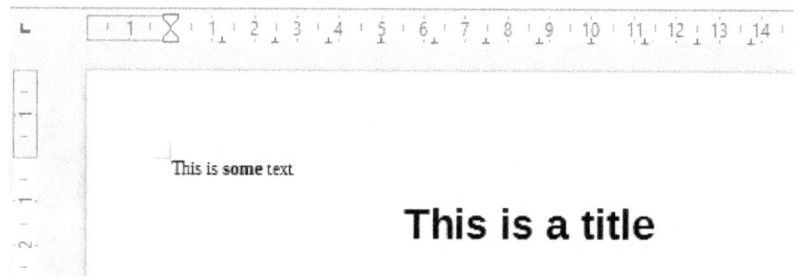

Once you've saved the file importing the document into your text frame is as simple as right clicking on the frame, choosing

 to get an Open dialogue.

Use the Look in box to go to the directory where you saved the file.

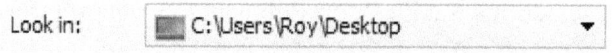

Then double click on it from the list of files:

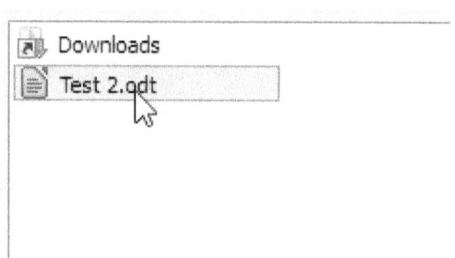

You'll see a warning. Note that it won't be easy to recover any text that you lose at this stage. So be careful before clicking on Yes because you don't want to lose anything that matters.

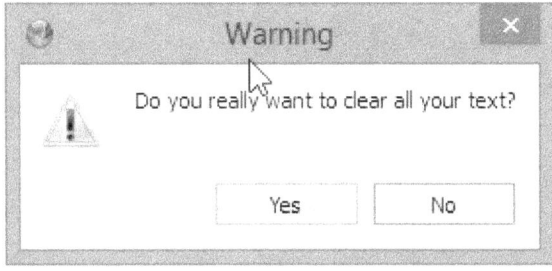

Once you click on Yes you'll see the OpenDocument Importer.

This offers you the option of overwriting existing paragraph styles – so if the current documents has the same style as the imported document, Scribus will change the style to match the imported document. The next window will allow you to control how Scribus imports the document.

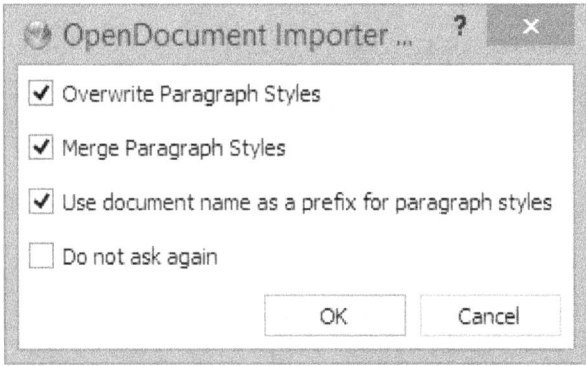

Overwriting Paragraph Styles will change the appearance of other parts of the document. So you need to be careful when using it.

Merge Paragraph Styles will combine together styles that have the same properties. Occasionally, though, there might be a reason why you've called two styles a different name so be a little careful.

The final option means that Scribus will use the document name as the prefix for the paragraph style. So, a style might be called something like Test 2_Index if your file name is Test 2.

⊿ Paragraph Styles
   Default Paragraph Style
   Test 2_Index
   Test 2_Text_20_body
   Test 2_Title

Click [OK] to continue.

You'll see the imported text in the Text Frame.

This is **some** text

This is a title

One thing that can happen is that the file that you import contains more text than the text frame you're importing the text to can handle. For example, see below:

This is **some** text

This is a title

This is some random text. There's going to be a lot of it:

celerisque, dapibus a, consequat at, leo.

Pellentesque libero lectus, tristique ac, consectetuer sit amet, imperdiet ut, justo. Sed aliquam odio vitae

Note that at the bottom right hand corner of the text frame there is a little cross in a box ⊞ which indicates that the text frame contains more text that it can display.

Resizing Text Frames

Text Frames are handled by Scribus in the same way as objects are in most modern programs. When you click on them you'll see small red rectangles on each corner and the middle of each edge. To resize them move the mouse to one of the rectangles, click and hold the mouse, and then move it towards or away from the centre to make it larger or smaller.

The rectangles in the middle of an edge only move that edge, while the rectangles at the corner move both edges.

Sometimes, you'll find that resizing a Text Frame to make it larger is enough to allow it to display all of its contents. When that doesn't work you may need to insert another Text Frame.

Linking Text Frames on the Same Page

We've already discussed how to Insert a Text Frame. If you think about a newspaper, it's a common thing for an article to start in one place in a page or document and then concluded in another place. If we had to manually mess around with moving the text every time we changed the layout slightly things would become very complicated.

But Scribus has a technique called Linking.

This acts a little like an overflow buffer. When you link a frame and excess text from one frame goes to the next.

Once you've added the second frame the next step is to select the frame with excess text by clicking on it.

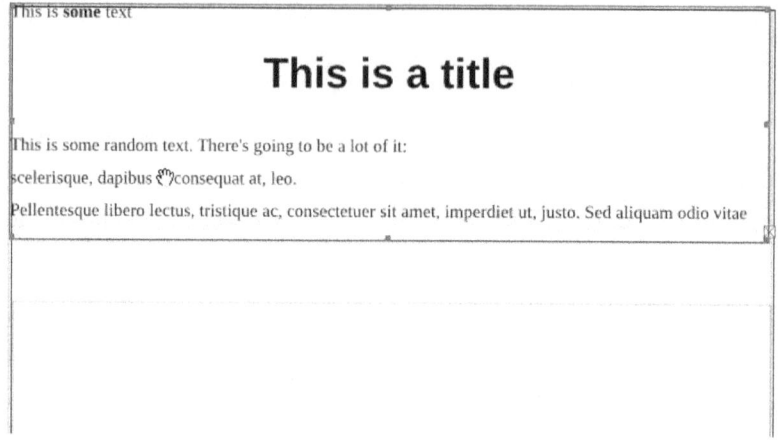

Then, click on the link frames icon 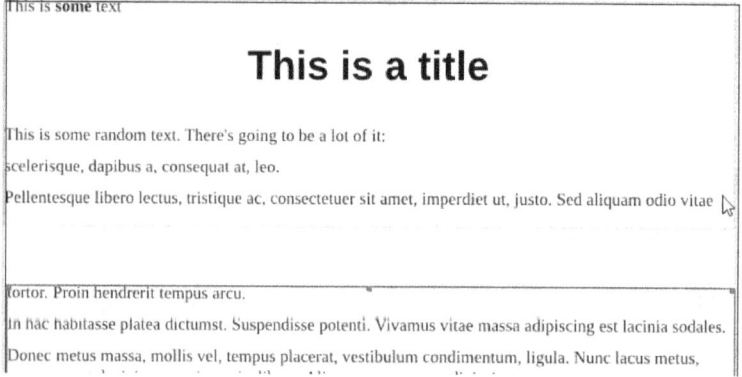 in the toolbar. You'll see

the mouse pointer change . Move the mouse to the destination frame and click. You'll see the text appear in the destination frame.

One thing to be careful of is the fact that the destination Frame may not contain enough space to display everything that you want to display.

And sometimes you might even run out of space in the document. For example, in the current document you've only got one page. And that might not be enough.

Inserting a New Page

The Pages menu contains most of the functionality that Scribus has for manipulating the pages of a document. To insert a new page, click on Insert in the Pages menu.

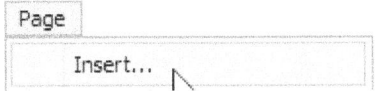

We'll discuss most of these options in much more detail later on, but for the moment the only thing to be aware of is at the top. Changing the number of pages we're going to insert. In this case, I don't know how many pages I'm going to need so I've chosen to insert a lot of pages.

I can delete any unwanted pages later.

Finally I click [OK] .

Page Navigation

Note that at the bottom of the screen you can now see a navigation icon. [1 ∨ of 15] we are currently on the first page of 15. If you click on you go to the next page. Note that the greyed out back arrow becomes green. [2 ∨ of 15] you can go back a page using the arrow, go to the start by clicking on or the end by clicking on . You can even type a number into the box [5 ∨] and click enter to go to a specific page.

In addition you can scroll through the entire document using the scroll bar on the right.

When you scroll through a document in this way you can often see two pages at once.

urna, interdum vel, ultricies vel, faucibus at, quam.

Donec elit est, consectetuer eget, consequat quis, tempus quis, wisi. In in nunc. Class aptent taciti sociosqu ad litora torquent per conubia nostra, per inceptos hymenaeos.

Donec ullamcorper fringilla eros. Fusce in sapien eu purus dapibus commodo. Cum sociis natoque penatibus et magnis dis parturient montes, nascetur ridiculus mus.

Linking Frames on Multiple Pages

We've already covered how to link a frame on a single page. Well, it's not that different linking frames across multiple pages.

First use the page navigation methods described above to go to the destination page. For example, if you want to continue on Page 3, type 3 into the box: and press enter.

Then insert the Text Frame in the page. (Remember, Insert Text Frame   T   in the Insert Menu)

Return to the page with the Frame with the excess text. In this case it's page 1 so type and press enter or click on . Click on the Origin frame, then on the Link Frames icon in the toolbar.

Go back to page and click on the empty frame. Congratulations, you've linked the two frames together.

Note that you can repeat the process as often as needed – i.e. until you're displaying all of the text.

Setting the Default Document Font

Obviously as you create frames you can assign different Fonts to the text in them. But when you're working with a large document assigning a style to every paragraph can be time consuming and inefficient.

By default every time you add a Frame the text has no style. It is displayed in the default document font.

This Text Frame is only the default font.

The vast amount of text in most documents should be the default font. You don't want to use hundreds of different fonts throughout a document. They generally look better if you have a standard font choice for basic text, and other styles for a limited number of purposes that are consistent throughout the document.

But of course you can change the default font. And when you do, all the text like the above will change at the same time.

To do this click on Styles... F3 in the Edit menu. Click on Default Paragraph Style on the list.

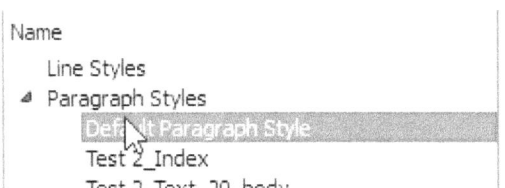

And then click on Edit >> to open the edit style window. Click on the Character Style tab. The options that you are most likely to use are the font choice option.

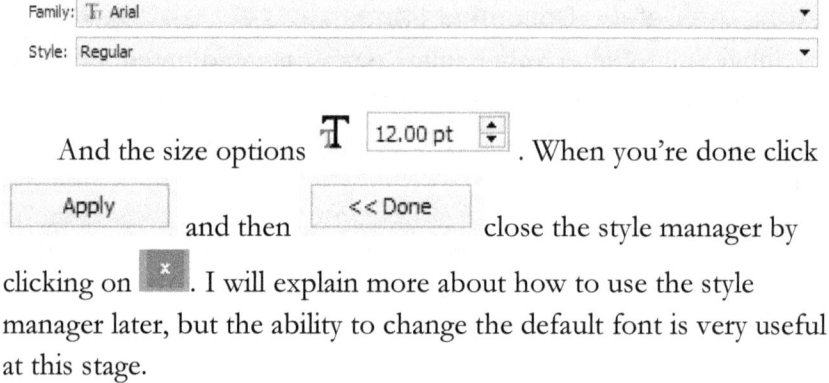

And the size options . When you're done click

and then close the style manager by

clicking on . I will explain more about how to use the style manager later, but the ability to change the default font is very useful at this stage.

Checking Spelling

You'll often want to Check Spelling for words in a text frame. Make sure you've selected the text frame and then click on

> Check Spelling…   Shift+F7   in the Item menu.

For example, given this text frame:

> This is some texxt with an errorr

Click onto the frame to select it, and when you run the spell check a dialogue window will open. I find that it can take a little while for this to happen. Scribus will automatically detect the language.

> Text Language: English (UK) ▼

You can change this option if you want. It will then run through the entire text frame from top to bottom. When it finds an error it will highlight it in red:

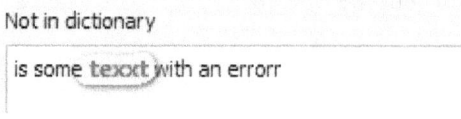

And will offer some suggestions:

You can choose to ignore the error once or every time that Scribus finds it.

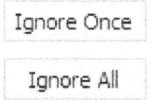

You can either click on a suggestion and then choose to change it just the once, or change it throughout the text frame.

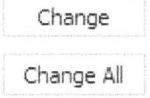

When it's done it'll display Spelling check complete at the bottom of the screen.

One of the reasons I suggest writing documents in a word processor first and then importing them into Scribus later is that the spell check process is irritating in Scribus because you run a spell check on each frame individually.

Handling Text

When you're working with text in a text frame there several operations that you'll often have to select text. One of the easiest ways to do this is to click into the text frame close to the point that you're editing, move the mouse to the end of the text you want to select, click and hold the mouse then move to the beginning of the text that you want to select.

You'll see the text highlighted.

ibero lectus, tristique ac, consectetu
mperdiet ut, justo. Sed aliquam odic
ıendrerit tempus arcu.

Once you've highlighted text you can delete it by pressing the
backspace key, or replace it by typing whatever text you want to
replace it by. You can also use operations to move the text around.
These operations are pretty standard in other programs – cut, copy,
and paste. You'll have come across them before.

Cut

When you cut you take a copy of the text or object and then
delete it from the document. Select the text that you want to cut, then
press ✂ Cut   Ctrl+X   in the Edit menu.
Note that Scribus will remember the text that you cut.

Copy

When you copy something you put it on the clipboard (i.e.
remember it) but you don't delete it. Select the text or the object you
want to copy, then press ⧉ Copy   Ctrl+C   in
the Edit menu.

Paste

Pasting involves taking the most recent thing that you stored in
the clipboard and putting it into the document. Like all of these
options you can do it on an entire object (such as an image, shape
etc.) or a part of the text. If you're pasting text go to the place in the
document where you want to paste it, then press
▯ Paste   Ctrl+V   in the Edit Menu.

Clearing the Contents of a Frame

To clear the contents of a text frame right click on the frame,
hover your mouse over contents and click on clear.

You'll normally see a warning that tells you that you're deleting the contents. Click OK. Remember that this is a permanent option – you won't be able to change your mind later on!

Deleting

To delete an object select it first, and then press the delete (sometimes del) key on your keyboard. Note that this option is often not undoable. So, be careful before you decide to delete something.

Moving an Object

To move an object you can click on it, hold the mouse button, and move the mouse pointer to the place that you want the object to go. You'll see a ghost image of the object which shows you exactly where the image will go when you move it.

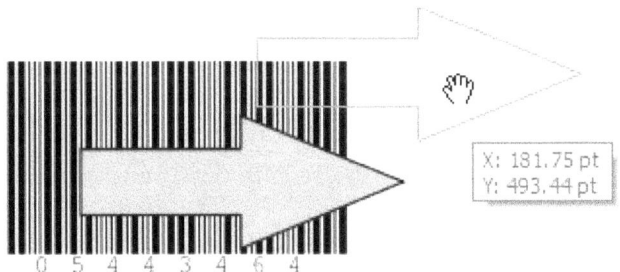

Let go of the mouse to complete the move. If you change your mind about moving the image simply right click with the mouse instead of letting go.

Undo

Scribus does offer an Undo facility. You can use Ctrl+Z to undo, and Ctrl+Y to redo. Unfortunately I find that the undo and redo facility that Scribus offers isn't as good as other programs. Often things that you'd have thought should be Undoable aren't. For example, sometimes moving text frames or objects can't be undone.

I suggest as a general rule making sure that you save your document frequently.

Search

To search through a text frame you must select the text frame first. Then click on  in the edit menu.

For people that are used to the default search method in programs like word this can be a bit intimidating. However, the default option of selecting text means that you can just type in the text to be searched for into the box

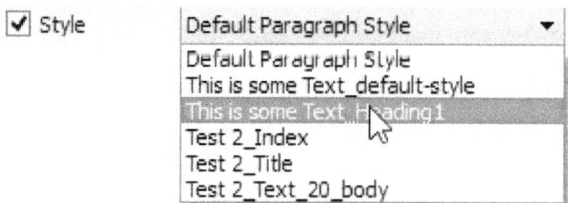

The search dialogue is much more powerful. By clicking on the ☐ beside any option you can choose to search for your setting for that option. Clicking on ☑ will toggle (turn) off that option.

So with the following you've decided to search by style and then click the value combo box by the style to determine which style to search through.

When you're searching think of it as an AND search. So you'll only find text that matches all the options that you have selected.

Press ⬚Search⬚ to find text that matches the options

that you've selected. The first item in the Text Field that matches

your criterion will be highlighted. Press `Search` again to
find the next item. When there are no more items that match the
search string to be found you'll see a message like:

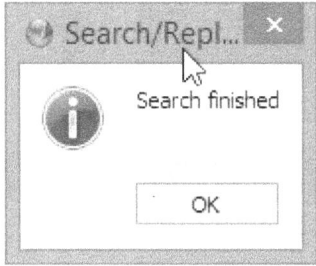

Replace

Replace works in a very similar way to Search. For example if
you are searching for

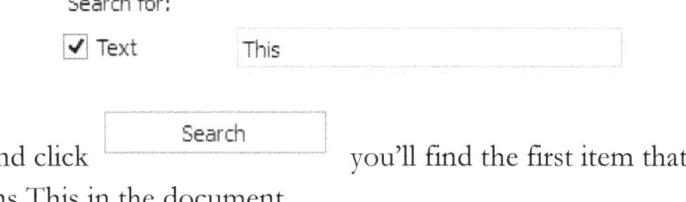

And click `Search` you'll find the first item that
contains This in the document.

If you choose to replace the text with

Replace with:
✔ Text   That
—

And hit `Replace` then the item that has been found by
search will be replaced by your selection and the search will go to the
next item. You can choose not to replace an item by clicking on

`Search` rather than replace.

Of course you can replace every instance of a search criteria by using 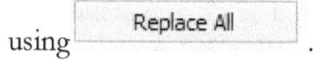 .

In a way the above is the most basic way that you can use Replace. It's the other options that make it so powerful. For example, if you want to change all instances of a style to another style to another frame you might search for:

Search for:

☐ Text   This

☑ Style   Test 2_Title ▼

And replace it with:

Replace with:

☐ Text   That

☑ Style   Default Paragraph Style ▼

In the same way as you could with Search you can choose what features to alter in the replace by clicking on the ☐ to toggle a replace option on, or the ☑ to toggle it off.

Once you try these options out you'll find out how powerful they are.

Selecting

We've already shown you that single clicking an object selects it. You get a red border around the object.

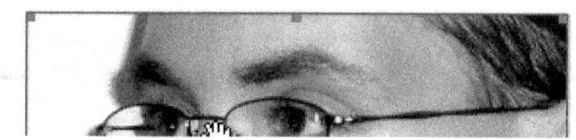

Once you've selected a text frame you can click anywhere within the text to start editing it. Or you can highlight (in other words select) text by going to the end of the text you want to select, holding the mouse button down then moving the mouse pointer to the beginning of the text).

There are some other options that you might want to be aware of. When you want to select all the objects on the page you can click Select All Ctrl+A in the edit menu. If you've selected an object that you didn't want to select you can click Deselect All Ctrl+Shift+A in the edit menu, or simply in the grey area around the page (as long as you don't have an object where you're going to click!)

Advanced Select All

Sometimes you may want more control over the objects that you select. For example, you may want to select only text frames or image frames. You can use Advanced Select All... Ctrl+Alt+A in the Edit menu to run a selective select all (that's a mouthful!).

When you run the Advanced Select All you'll see an option that determines where you will select the objects from.

⦿ on Current Page　　　○ on Current Layer　　　○ on the Scratch Space

I'll discuss the scratch area below, and Layers later on in the book. But since everything that you've done so far is on the Current Page you can leave this choice as it is.

If you click the rectangle next to ☐ With the Following Attributes to toggle it on (or, in other words, to turn it on) you can then choose objects of certain types:

To do this with any of the options click on the rectangle ☐ .

Although most of these options are relatively obvious for the moment the main thing that we've seen is object or item type. If you select it you'll see that you can choose between Text Frame and

Image Frame and other objects that we haven't used yet.

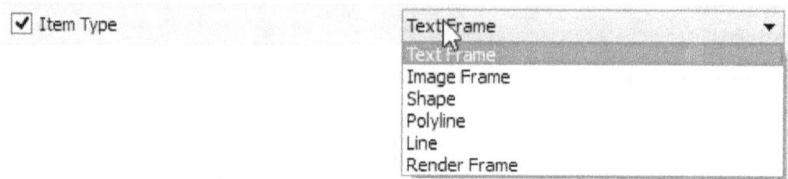

As you go through this book you'll find more and more of the options make sense. For example, in the shape tutorial you'll learn all about Fill Colour, and in the Object Tutorial you'll learn about locking and resizable properties.

Scratch Area

When you're editing a document you may not be sure that you want to remove an object without deleting it altogether. Around the document there is a grey area that is called the scratch space. This area can contain images that won't be printed out with the document but which are saved for future use.

For example if you drag and drop an image into the scratch area:

Then run a print preview you'll see that the image has disappeared from the page that would be printed out. But when you're editing the file you can put the image back onto the document by simply dragging and dropping it on.

4 INSERTING IMAGES

So far we've inserted one type of object. A Text Frame. While this is a very useful type of object it's not going to make the most beautiful design. Another type of object that is very common is an Image Object. This is, in essence, a photograph or illustration.

Obviously, you'll use another application to create or edit your picture. I've described one such application in my book Use Magix Photo Editor, but there are dozens of other applications including Gimp.

Inserting an Image Frame

The method for inserting an Image Frame is very like the way you'd insert a Text Frame. Click on  in the Insert Menu. The mouse will change to:

Then draw the Image Frame in the same way that you'd draw a Text Frame. One thing to note is that even though we've already got an object – a text frame – where we are drawing the Image Frame this doesn't stop us adding a Frame "on top" of the existing object.

That's pretty much the case for all Frames.

elerisque, dapibus a, consequat at, leo.

ıllentesque libero lectus, tristique ac, consectetuer sit amet, imperd

ırtor. Proin hendrerit tempus arcu.

ı hac habitasse platea dictumst. Suspendisse potenti. Vivamus vitaı

ıonec metus massa, mollis vel, tempus place Width: 134.25 pt ı condin
ɔsuere eget, lacinia eu, varius quis, libero. A Height: 82.50 pt my adiɲ

Once you adjust the mouse to the right shape you'll see the new Frame:

is is some random text. There's going to be a lot of it:

ılerisque, dapibus a, consequat at, leo.

llentesque libero lectus, tristique ac, consectetuer sit amet, imperdiet uı

rtor. Proin hendrerit tempus arcu.

hac habitasse platea dictumst. Suspendisse potenti. Vivamus vitae mas

ınec metus massa, mollis vel, tempus placerat, vestibulum condimentu

For the moment it's empty. So we'd better add an image to the Frame.

Show Grid

So far we've been quite freewheeling where it comes to laying out, doing everything by eye. But Scribus provides a few features that make it easier to place objects. One of these features is the Grid. This is a square which allows you to more accurately place objects.

To Show the Grid click on 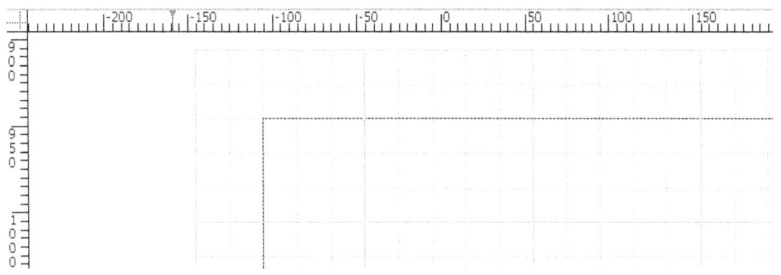 in view. You'll see some additional lines on the document.

When you're inserting frames into the document you can use these lines to place objects at regular distances from each other. For example, we've got two Text Frames both of identical size and placement below:

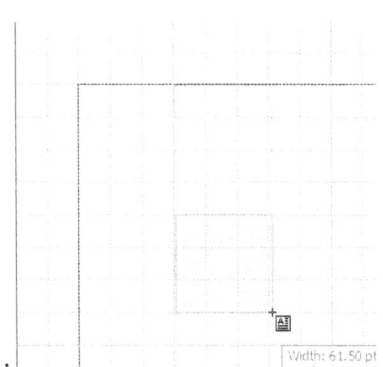

You can hide the grid by clicking Show Grid in the Window menu for a second time.

Snapping to the Grid

When you're inserting objects it's possible to set an option that forces the object to line up to the grid. This is called "Snapping to the Grid". When you're inserting an object close to the grid, Scribus will move the object to the Grid Line.

To enable this functionality click 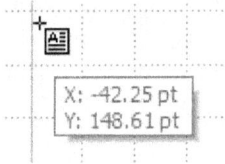 in the Page menu. Say you start inserting an object here. Note it's not actually on the grid:

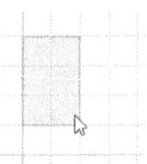

When you start drawing the frame will always match the Grid.

You can turn it off by clicking the again in the Page Menu.

Changing the Size of the Grid

When you're snapping to the Grid large grid sizes like the above can be difficult to manage. Fortunately it's possible to change the default Grid size in Scribus.

First, click on **Document Setup...** in the File menu.

Click on Guides in the frame on the left of the document setup dialogue. Note that there is a Major Grid which is the large square, and a minor grid which is the smaller squares. Change the point size to make the spacing of the grid smaller or larger.

Spacing: 100.00 pt

Once you've finished making the changes click   OK   to
apply them and close the dialogue.

As a rule I find that changing the Minor Grid is better than the
Major Grid, since reducing that to a smaller figure gives you a lot of
control without losing the big picture that you gain from the Major
Grid.

Adding an Image to the Frame

Probably the most common way to add an Image to the Frame
is to right click on it and then

select   Get Image...   Ctrl+I   . This will display an
open dialogue. You can change the directory in the normal way by
clicking on the

Look in: C:\Users\Roy\Google Drive\Tom\NEA   box, or you can
use the directory list to the right. Once you're in the right directory
single click on the file to display a preview:

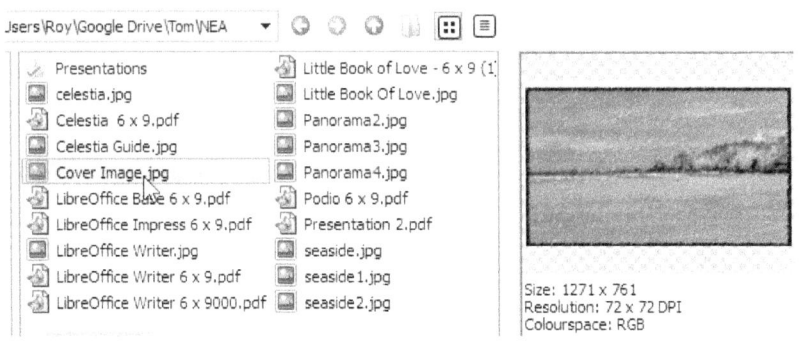

Then click   OK   when you're happy that you've selected
the right Image. Note that when you click OK you'll lose anything
you had in the Frame prior to Getting the Image.

Here's a look at the result of these actions:

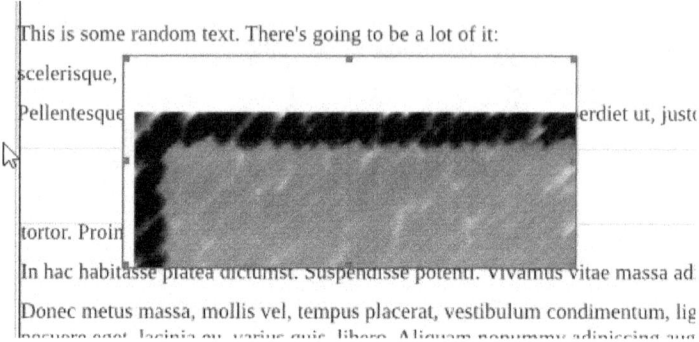

There are two main problems here. First, the Text doesn't flow around the Image. And, Secondly the Image doesn't really fit the Frame. There are two ways we can solve this. Change the Frame to suite the Image, or change the Image to suit the Frame.

Adding a PDF File to the Frame

The steps to add a PDF file to an Image Frame are basically the same as the steps needed to insert an Image into the Image File. Create the Image Frame first then double click on it. Make sure that the file of type combo box is set to include all types:

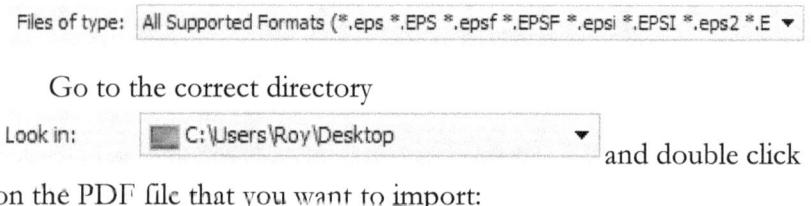

Go to the correct directory

Look in: C:\Users\Roy\Desktop and double click on the PDF file that you want to import:

While Scribus can add a PDF file to the frame it doesn't easily allow you to edit the PDF file. You must do this in your PDF editor of choice.

Resizing the Frame to Fit the Image

In an ideal world we'd always resize the Frame rather than the Image. An image is almost always better at the original size rather than either shrunk or enlarged. This is the case especially when you're enlarging the image. The reason for this is that if you make an image larger on the screen you aren't adding more data about what the image should look like. So instead of just depicting 1 pixel, the same information is used to depict more than one. You end up with a blocky look that just doesn't particularly look like the original image.

Resizing the Frame to Fit the Image is simply a case of right clicking on the Frame and

selecting 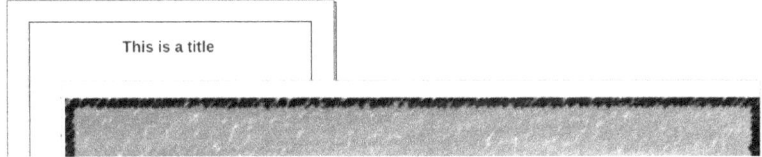. The problem is sometimes the Image is just too large for the document:

This is a title

In these cases you have to adjust the Image to Fit the Frame.

Fitting the Image to the Frame – Simple Method

Right click on the Frame and then

on . There. That's done:

que, dapibus a, consequat at, leo.

sque   r sit amet, imperdiet ut,

'roin

iabit   nti. Vivamus vitae mass

metus massa, mollis vel, tempus placerat, vestibulum condimentum

Fitting the Image to the Frame – Complex Method

Scribus allows you a slightly finer control over how the Image is adjusted to the Frame than the last section suggests. Often you won't need to use these methods. But sometimes they are valuable. If you right click on the Image Frame and

Properties   F2

you'll see the Properties Dialogue.

This controls many of the ways that the Image Frame acts and interacts with other Objects.

You can control how the image is scaled through clicking on the

Image

button in the Properties window. At the moment you're on Free Scaling mode. Because the image hasn't been scaled yet it is at 100%.

Free Scaling

X-Pos:	0.00 pt
Y-Pos:	0.00 pt
X-Scale:	100.00 %
Y-Scale:	100.00 %
Actual X-DPI:	72.00
Actual Y-DPI:	72.00

If you change the X-Scale it will adjust the image horizontally, either larger or smaller as a percentage. For example

X-Scale: 10.00 %

results in an image like:

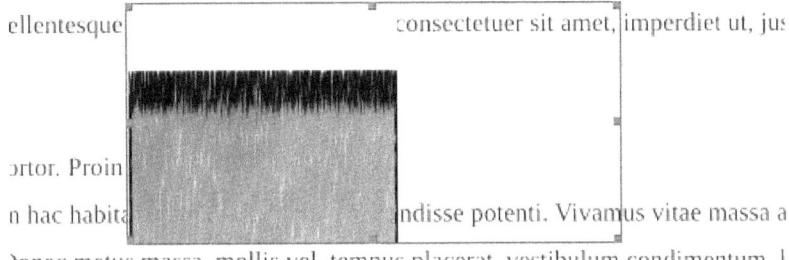

his is some random text. There's going to be a lot of it:

:elerisque, dapibus a, consequat at, leo.

ellentesque consectetuer sit amet, imperdiet ut, jus

ɔrtor. Proin

n hac habitɑ ndisse potenti. Vivamus vitae massa a

)onec metus massa, mollis vel, tempus placerat, vestibulum condimentum, l

If you adjust the Y-Scale it will alter the image vertically. For example:

X-Scale: 100.00 %

Y-Scale: 10.00 %

Results in the following Image:

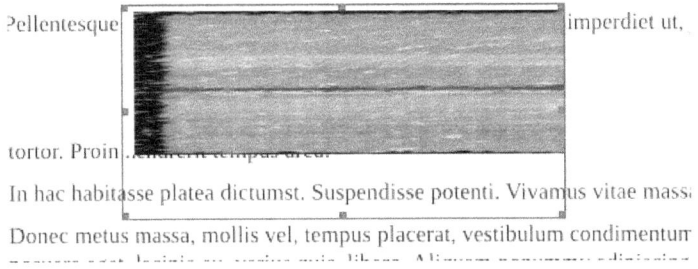

This is some random text. There's going to be a lot of it:

;celerisque, dapibus a, consequat at, leo.

Pellentesque imperdiet ut,

tortor. Proin

In hac habitasse platea dictumst. Suspendisse potenti. Vivamus vitae massɑ

Donec metus massa, mollis vel, tempus placerat, vestibulum condimentum

When you use this slightly more complicated way of scaling the image you have a lot of control. And with control comes the ability to alter the image in ways that distort it. As you can see above, keeping the X-Scale and Y-Scale percentage the same will make sure the image remains proportional. If you adjust them to different percentages the "aspect ratio" will be altered which means one side of the image will appear longer or shorter than the other side.

Or, in other words, the image may appear silly

Resizing an Image to Get an Apparent DPI

As a Desk Top Publishing Program Scribus has been designed to allow you to create PDF documents for books. Most printers requite 300 dpi or above for all images. You can use the scale functionality to make sure that an image has the right DPI for the printer.

For convenience it's wise to click on the Lock option, so that both X and Y DPI are adjusted at once.

Type the DPI you want the end image to be into the provided box:

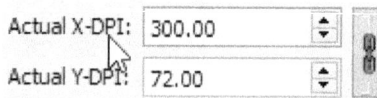

When you click out of the box, you'll see the other DPI box, but also the X-Scale and Y-Scale boxes change. The image will also shrink so the effective DPI is 300.

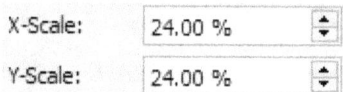

If you still need to shrink the image further just click on and adjust the DPI figure again.

One thing about this that might be of interest to you. As you shrink the X-Scale you'll see the Actual X-DPI got up, and as you enlarge it the X-DPI will go down. This is because DPI (dots per inches) is directly related to the size of the image. As you reduce the size you increase the amount of dots per inches that Scribus can draw.

Resizing an image does NOT affect the basic image, just the

depiction of it. Reducing or increasing the number of dots or pixels that Scribus can display for every inch of screen or paper space.

Scale to Frame Size

If you select  Scribus will automatically fit the image into the frame in the most effective way that it can:

ˑisque, dapibus a, consequat at, leo.

ɪtesque   r sit amet, imperdiet ut

r. Proin

c habita   nti. Vivamus vitae mas

ɩc metus massa, mollis vel, tempus placerat, vestibulum condimentu

ɒre eget lacinia eu varius quis libero Aliquam nonummy adipiscir

Noting of course that unless you remove the tick by

☑ Proportional it will maintain the aspect ratio of the image.

Make Text Wrap Around an Image.

When you've got an image that is on top of a text frame the default behaviour is for LibreOffice to just put the image on top of the text. You've seen an example of this above. You can change this behaviour in the properties window (right click on the frame and

select 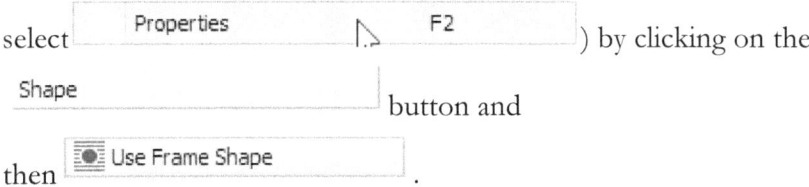) by clicking on the

Shape button and

then [■] Use Frame Shape .

, is some random text. There's going to be a lot of it:

erisque,   dapibus a, c

entesque   libero lectus

et,   imperdiet ut

or. Proin   hendrerit tei

iac habitasse platea dictumst. Suspendisse potenti. Vivamus vitae mass

This can often work best if you manually resize the Frame using the same method as the text box (i.e. clicking on the red rectangle on the edge, holding the mouse down, and dragging the mouse close to the edge of the actual image). Doing this will remove some of the white space in the text box:

This is some random text. There's going to be a lot of it:

scelerisque,   dapibus a, cc

Pellentesque   libero lectus,

Imperdiet ut,   justo. Sed ali
tempus arcu.

In hac habitasse platea dictumst. Suspendisse potenti. Vivamus v

Adding space around the Image

While we've already show you how to wrap text around an image sometimes people want some white space around the image so the image doesn't flow into the text. The first step to achieve this goal is to adjust the contour line of the image.

First, right click on the image frame and make sure that you adjust the frame to the image:

Adjust Frame to Image  so that there is no empty space in the frame. (You may have had to Adjust the Image to the Frame first if the image was too large for the frame that you chose).

Now we need to adjust the contour line of the frame. Click on Shape in the Image Properties. Then click on Edit. Shape: Edit... .

You'll see the Edit Shape dialogue.

Click on the rectangle by Edit Contour Line .

You can either choose to increase the contour line by a fixed (absolute) value or a percentage. Obviously change the number in the text field to change the exact amount you're increasing it.

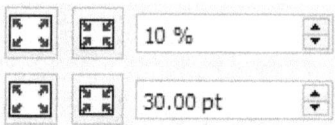

Either way to increase the contour click on [icon]. You'll see a blue line around the image. This is the Contour line. It's now outside the image.

You can adjust the contour line further and when you're happy click on End Editing .

The jobs only half done! Nothing's changed! And it won't until you're using the contour line. Click on

Use Contour Line to wrap text around the contour line.

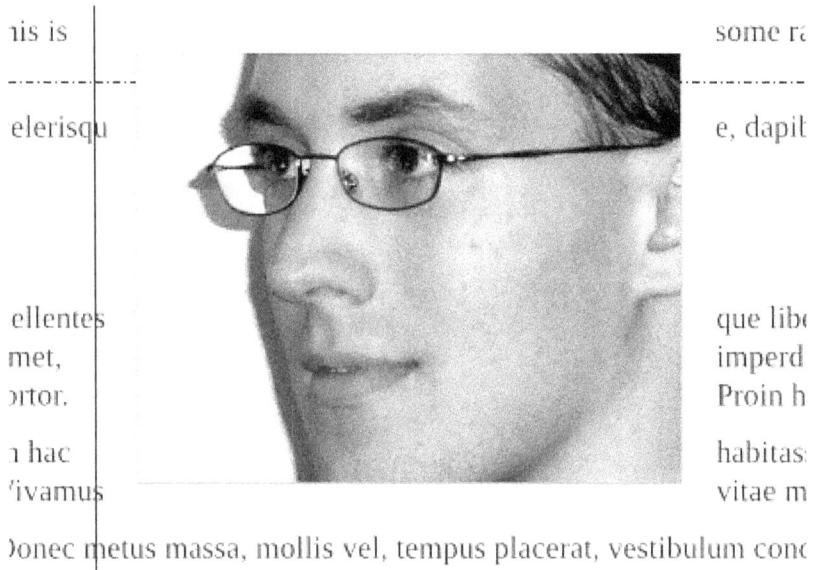

iis is ⋮ some rɛ

elerisqu ⋮ e, dapil

ellentes ⋮ que libɛ
met, ⋮ imperd
ɔrtor. ⋮ Proin h
ɪ hac ⋮ habitas:
ʼivamus ⋮ vitae m

)onec metus massa, mollis vel, tempus placerat, vestibulum conc

This seems quite complex at first but it's remarkable how quickly you get used to doing this. And it gives you a nice border around the image.

Locking the Size of an Object

While scaling an object so that it's the right size is something that can help you it's important to prevent accidental resizing. You can do this by locking the size of the frame.

In the Properties dockable window (which you opened in the last step) if necessary click on X, Y, Z to see the positon information for the image. This is the default opening section for the Properties window so sometimes you'll see it automatically.

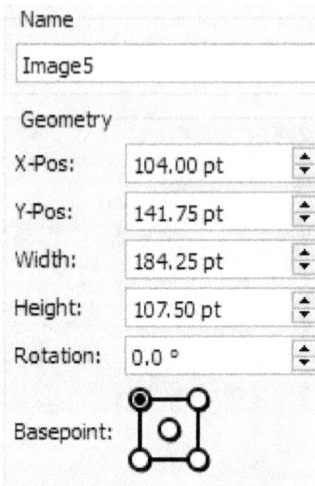

Below the location information you can see the X,Y,Z toolbar. Depending how large the Scribus main window is you may not see all the icons. In which case you might have to scroll across or down using the scroll bar:

You can lock or unlock the size of the object by clicking on ⊡ .

Updating an Image

Sometimes an image might appear to become "stuck". For example, if you change one of the Properties, or delete the image, you may be left with a frame that just doesn't look like it reflects the most current choices you've made for the image. If this is the case, right click on the frame then on Update Image .

Getting an Image by Pasting It into a Frame.

It would be awfully inconvenient if you had to save an image every time you wanted to cut and paste it from another program. But right click on an image frame and select

☐ Paste Image from Clipboard to paste the image directly into the Frame.

Text over an Image.

One of the things that people find hardest to understand sometimes about Scribus is the way levels work. Each object is assigned a level. For example in the document below both text frames are "below" the Image Frame.

While we can set the Image Frame Properties to force word wrapping around the image, there's no obvious way to make the text go over the image.

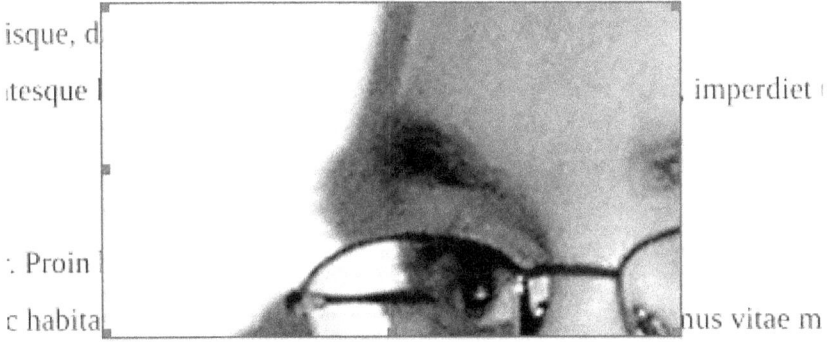

c metus massa, mollis vel, tempus placerat, vestibulum condimen

To make text go over the image we've got to lower the level of the image. You do this by right clicking on the Frame, and then hovering your mouse over Level. You can select Lower.

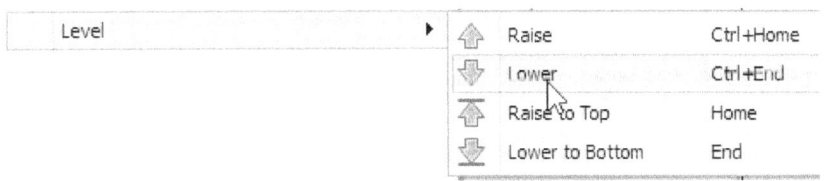

In this case, I'm just going to lower the Level one step:

is some random text. There's going to be a lot of it:

erisque, d

entesque l   imperdi

or. Proin hendrerit tempus arcu.

ac habitasse platea dictumst. Suspendisse potenti. Vivamus vitae

iec metus massa, mollis vel, tempus placerat, vestibulum condim

The Image is still at a higher level than one of the text frames, but at a lower level than the other in this case. If you lower it again as many times as necessary or click

Lower to Bottom   End   which puts the currently selected frame at the bottom of the pile, you'll see the result:

his is some random text. There's going to be a lot of it:

elerisque, dapibus a, consequat at, leo.

ellentesque libero lectus, tristique ac, consectetuer sit amet, impe

ortor. Proin hendrerit tempus arcu.

n hac habitasse platea dictumst. Suspendisse potenti. Vivamus vi

Donec metus massa, mollis vel, tempus placerat, vestibulum cond

These level settings work with most types of objects. Objects on a higher level hide objects on a lower level as a general rule.

You can alter this by right clicking on the image object and clicking 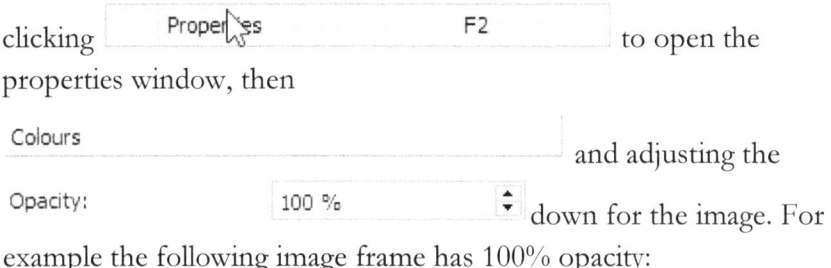 to open the properties window, then and adjusting the down for the image. For example the following image frame has 100% opacity:

But when we change it to we see that the lower level object is showing through the higher level:

Note that we can use the same procedure for most objects.

Naming an Object

In the X,Y,Z options you might have noticed an interesting field called Name. All objects have a name property. It can be quite useful to give an object a name that'll be obvious when you're using functions such as Outline (which we're just about to get to). So you know what the purpose of a particular control is.

Otherwise, Scribus just assigns a generic name that doesn't mean anything.

You can change the name of an object by opening the Properties dockable window, then clicking on X, Y, Z (if it isn't already open) and editing the Name field. Note that the Name Field can't contain spaces, and might prevent you using some special characters. I often like to start words (other than a) with a capital letter:

Name

PictureOfaPerson

Then, when you need to reference it at a later date you'll be able to remember what the control is actually called.

Outline

Sometimes you may not be able to select an object because another object is on top of it. There's an option called the Outline window that allows you to see and select all the objects on a page. To run it click on Outline in the Windows menu.

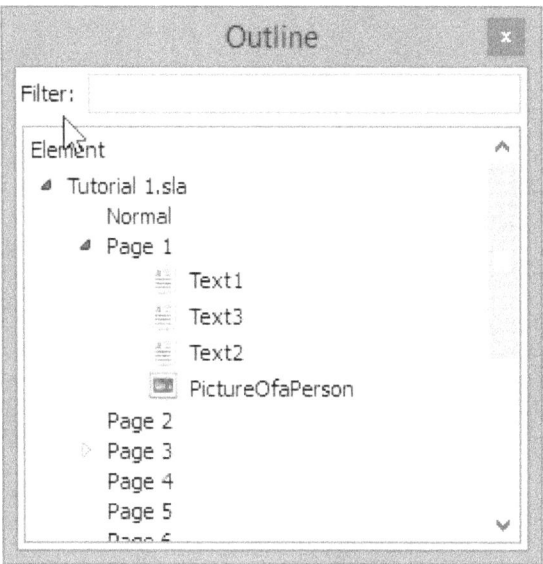

Notice that the entire document is included in the outline. Some of the Pages other than the current page may be collapsed. You'll see a ▷ symbol by these pages. If you click on the text (i.e. the name of the object) you will go to that object.

You can expand a section to show all the sub objects by clicking on the ▷.

To collapse the list just click on ◢.

In this section we've discussed some basic information on Image Frames. The next section will go on to giving more information about how to manage the document.

5 SAVING AND OPENING FILES.

New File

To create a new file click on

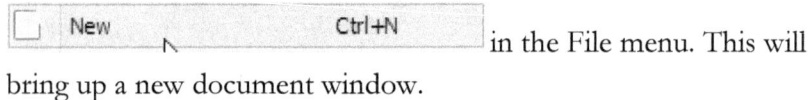 in the File menu. This will

bring up a new document window.

We've already seen this window before and explained most of the features. You can choose what layout, the paper size and orientation, the margins and bleeds, and the number of pages.

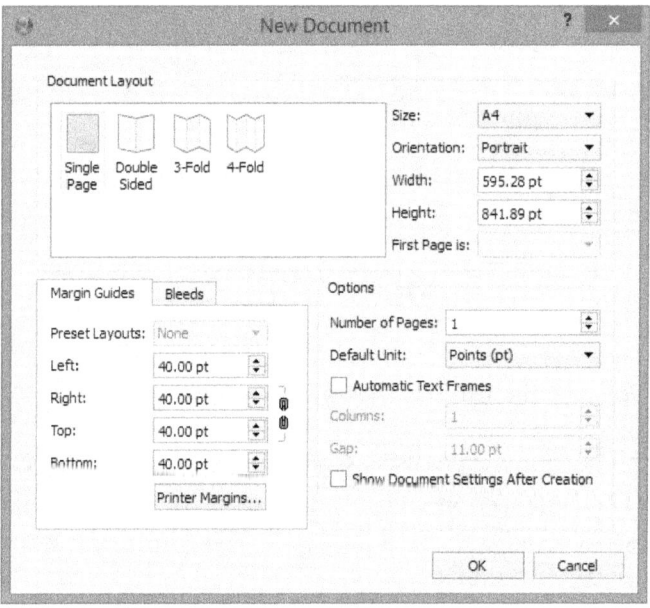

When you're happy with your choices click [OK] .

Saving

To save a file click on [Save   Ctrl+S] .
Scribus will save the file using the current file name unless it's the
first time that you've saved the file (i.e. it's a new document).

If it's a new document you'll see a Save As dialogue. Choose the
Directory as normal:

Look in: [C:\Users\Roy\Documents   ▼]

And then enter the File Name in the box provided:

File name: [Document-1.sla]

If you've already saved the file but want to give it a new name, or
save a backup file, you can use

[Save As...   Ctrl+Shift+S] in the File menu to bring up
the Save As dialogue.

Revert to Saved

Sometimes when you've edited a file you may want to revert to
the file as it was the last time you saved it. If you want to revert a file
click on [Revert to Saved] in the File Menu.

Closing a File

Before closing a file make sure that you've saved it, otherwise
you'll lose your work. Click on
[Close   Ctrl+F4] in the File Menu.

Opening File

Click on 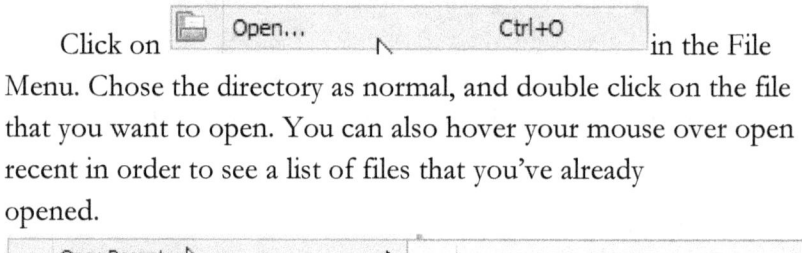 in the File Menu. Chose the directory as normal, and double click on the file that you want to open. You can also hover your mouse over open recent in order to see a list of files that you've already opened.

Moving Between Open Files

Scribus allows you to work on more than one file at a time. This can be useful when you want to cut and paste information from one document to another.

When you've got more than one file open at a time look at the bottom of the View menu and you'll see a list of the currently open files.

The file with the ✔ is the one that you're currently editing. If you click on one of the other files you'll see the Scribus window refresh to show the new file.

6 PRINTING DOCUMENTS

Obviously it's not much use to have a document that you can't print out. While Scribus provides a lot of export facilities that you can use to send the document to a commercial printing press it also has the ability to print out to your local printer like most other applications.

There is also a method of checking that the document that you're about to print or export is well formed (in other words, if there are any errors that would prevent you printing out the document) called the Preflight Verifier.

Preflight Verifier

To check the document doesn't contain any errors click on 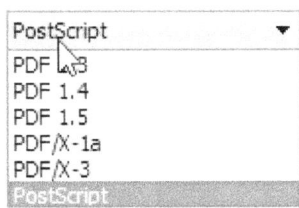 in the windows menu. Select the format that you want to check against. For example if you're printing out a PDF 1.5 document then you'd choose that profile.

When you're printing to your nearest printer it's generally best to choose PostScript.

Current Profile:

PostScript ▼
PDF 1.3
PDF 1.4
PDF 1.5
PDF/X-1a
PDF/X-3
PostScript

When you change the document or the current profile click on 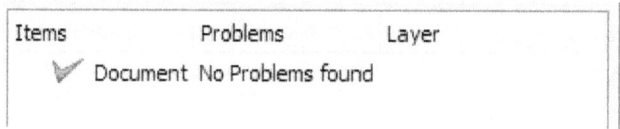 to run the verifier.

If the document doesn't contain any errors you'll see:

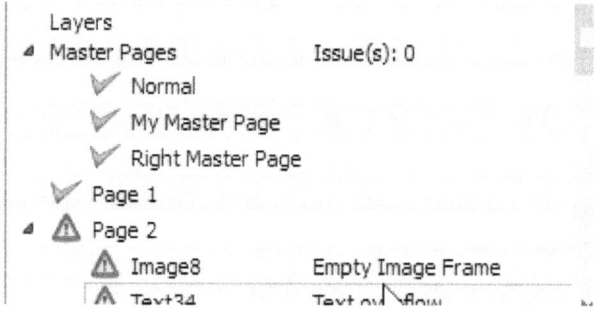

Otherwise you'll see a list of different pages in your document. Note that where something doesn't have a problem it has a ✔ by it.

Problems are indicated by ⚠. The name of the object or page is listed. And there is an error message that briefly describes the nature of the problem:

⚠ Page 2
⚠ Image8   Empty Image Frame

Clicking on a line will take you to the object that has a problem. You'll also see that the object is selected in the document.

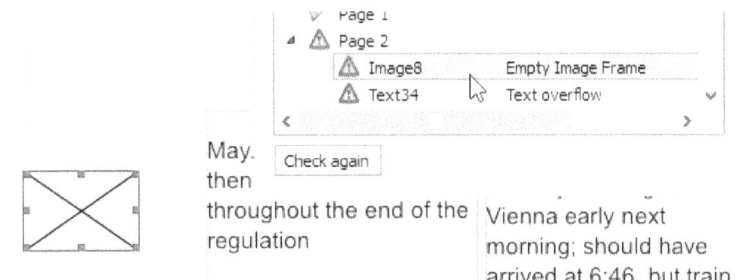

Once you've run through the entire document correcting errors

click on Check again to see if you've solved the problems.

Print Preview

Click on Print Preview   Ctrl+Alt+P   in the File
menu to run a print Preview. Scribus automatically runs the Preflight
Verifier when you print out the document. If there are no errors
you'll see the Print Preview window.

If there are errors you'll see the Preflight Verifier window. You

can chose to fix the problems or Ignore Errors but if you do chose to
ignore the problems then what you print might not reflect what you
actually wanted to print.

The Print Preview window is fairly obvious. You have a large
space that contains what the document will look like when you print
it out. Obviously, though, there will be variations in colour and image
resolution (a normal computer screen doesn't have the same
resolution as a printed document).

So the Print Preview won't give you a completely accurate
representation of what the document will look like. Just one that is
'good enough'.

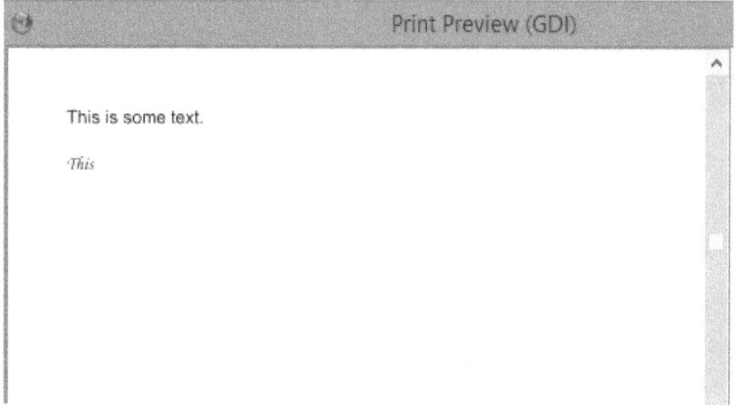

You can move between different pages of the document using the arrows at the bottom of the screen and reduce the size of the document in the preview using the scaling options.

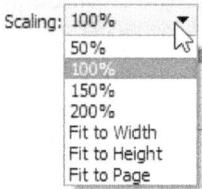

On the right tab are advanced options to change the colour profile of the document, and how the document handles transparencies, and also how it will handle margins and cropping.

When you're happy with your choices click on Print... .

The Print Dialogue will appear. See below for details about how to use it.

Print

You can run the Print Dialogue either through the Print Preview dialogue (see above) or by clicking in the toolbar, or

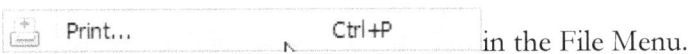 in the File Menu.

The first thing you will need to do is check that the Print Destination is correct. There's nothing worse than printing something to the wrong printer!

If you want to change the layout click on Options... to open the Printer Options dialogue. The options in this dialogue include how you collate the document, how many pages there are in print, and also some advanced options that you will only very rarely need to use.

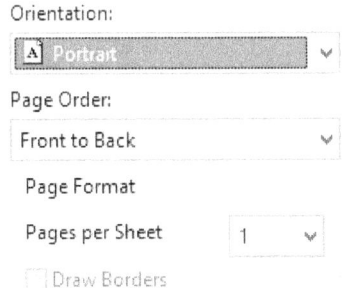

Then you can choose the pages to print. The main options are pretty standard. You can print all, the current page, or a page range. The page range is a comma separated list. For example: 1,3-4 would print out pages 1,3,4.

In the Print options you can choose to print in colour or greyscale:

Or use the options in the Advanced Options tab to control mirroring, under colour removal, and lots of other advanced features. You can also control Pre-Press features using Marks or page bleeds using Bleeds . For most users these options are very advanced and it's normally safe to keep them at the defaults unless you know specifically that you need to change them.

When you're happy with your choices press Print .

7 THE PAGES OF THE DOCUMENT

So far we've inserted two types of objects, and even managed few simple page based tasks – going from one page to another and inserting pages. Since Pages are an important part of the Scribus software package I'll cover some of the basics in this section.

As a rule before editing Pages I think it's a good idea to make sure that you backup or at least save your document first. Some of the changes you make can be permanent and not to your entire advantage. Being able to back out of them gracefully can save yourself an awful lot of hassle.

Insert Page

We've already covered inserting a page, but to remind you go to the page where you want to insert the Page using the page navigation toolbar. You can use the arrows (to go to the beginning, one page back, one page forward, or to the end) or type the page number into the box.

When you're at the right page click on

 in the Page menu to open the Insert Dialogue.

Previously we didn't use many of the settings in this dialogue. We saw that we could insert a set number of pages into the document by setting the  field. But it's possible to do more than that.

For example, say you want to insert a page in front of a particular page in the document. Just below the Insert Pages field there's an Insert Where box. When you click on it you can see the option to insert before Page or after Page.

In this case click before Page. You'll see that the greyed out field next to the Insert Where combo box becomes active once you've decided to insert before or after a page.

The value in this field is by default the page that you're currently editing. You can change the number to another page if you want to.

There is a Master Page field that I'll explain in the next section.

Documents can contain pages that are not the standard document format. So, a document that contains A4 pages might contain a few sheets that are A5. As a rule I recommend that all pages in the document SHOULD be the same size, but you can change the size of the page to a non-default value using the Page Size combo box.

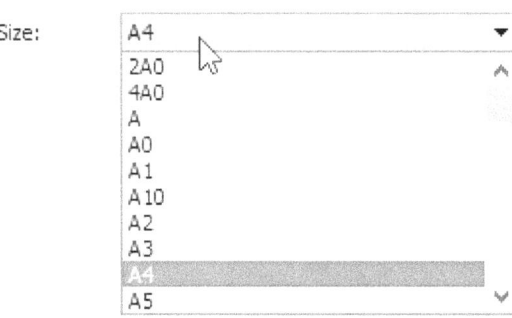

Related to this is the fact that when you scroll down you can select a custom size option.

This enables the Width and Height fields. You can choose the width and height of the document by editing them. You should be a little cautious when choosing a width and height this way, it's important to make sure that your printer can handle the size selected.

More frequently used is the Orientation box. This allows you to change a particular page so that it isn't in the standard Orientation you've chosen for your document. For example, you might display a map on one page that is landscape where all the other pages in your document is Portrait.

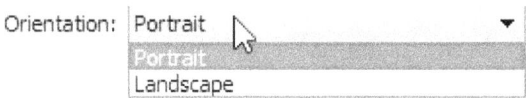

By default when you insert a new page either Before or After a specific page the objects on all subsequent pages (i.e. after the inserted page) are moved back on place.

For example, if you have pages 1,2,3,4 and insert a page X before page 2:1,X,3,4,5 the objects that were on Page 2 will now be on Page 3.

You can change this so the objects aren't shifted by deselecting ☑ Move Objects with their Page .

When you're happy with your choices click on [OK] .

Deleting a Page

Click on [Delete...] in the Pages Menu to delete a page. You'll see the Delete Pages dialogue which is pretty self-explanatory. It deletes pages From a number to a Number. Note that these pages are inclusive. So, 3 to 3 means you're going to delete page 3.

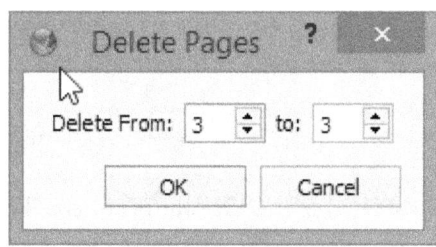

Whereas Delete From: 3 to: 5 means you'll delete pages 3,4 and 5.

Before you click OK it's important to remember that you're deleting the contents of the pages, and this change is basically permanent. So, save a backup of the document in case you change your mind at a later date.

Copying a Page

When you want to copy the objects on a page you can use this feature. One thing to note is that the contents of an object may be copied, but links won't be. So, if you copy page 1 in our tutorial the first text frame will be copied with all its content, and will link to the other text frames in the same page, but they won't link to Frames in pages in the document. You'll see that the bottom text frame has and overflow marker at the bottom right hand side.

Donec ullamcorper fringilla eros. Fusce in sapien eu purus dapibus commodo. Cum sociis natoque penatibus et magnis dis parturient montes, nascetur ridiculus mus.

You can copy the page by clicking on

Copy... in the Pages menu.

The first option sets the page to

copy Copy Page: 1 and is by default the page that you're currently editing.

The second option is the number of copies that you're going to make Number of Copies: 1 .

As with Insert you can choose where in the Document to copy the pages to.

At End
Before Page
After Page
At End

1

When you press OK Scribus will copy the Pages.

Move a Page

Click on Move... in the Pages menu to move a page. The first time you use this dialogue you may be slightly confused because the field:

Move Page(s): 1 To: 1

Is actually a range field. So, in this case you're moving page 1, and if you set it to 1 to 3 you'd be moving pages 1,2 and 3 rather than moving page 1 to location 1 in the document.

It's the next field that determines where the pages are moved to.

Just like Insert, Copy etc. you can choose to move the pages to the End, or before or after a page in the document.

Arranging Pages

Although you can move and delete pages as above sometimes it's helpful to have a way of visually moving them. You can do this by opening the Arranging Pages window. Click on

Arrange Pages   in the Windows menu.

There are two main sections in this window. The first is the Master Pages section that I'll explain later on. The second main section is the document Pages section:

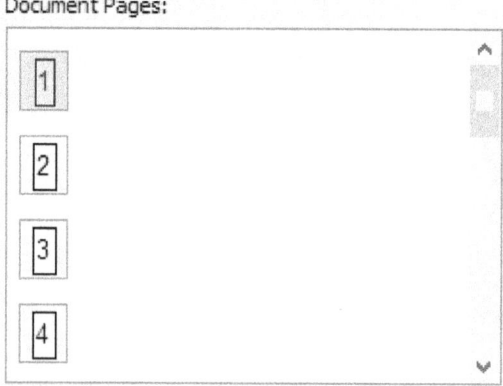

The page you're currently editing is highlighted e.g. ![1] . Click on another page to go to it.

To move a page first click on it and hold the mouse button, then drag the mouse up or down the list.

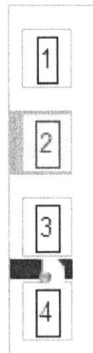

There's a visual indicator of where you're moving the pages to .

To delete a page click on the page and hold the mouse button.

Move the mouse to the bin .You'll see that as you move it the

mouse pointer changes to .

Importing Page(s)

When editing large documents you'll often work with groups of pages in separate files. For example, when producing a book you might have a document with an About the Author page and Back Matter which you only import into the final book when you've finished doing the rest of the work.

To import a page click on Import... in the Pages menu.

While it's theoretically possible to type the file name of the file you're going to import into the From Document: box, you'll generally browse for it by clicking on Select... and using the file open dialogue.

The page range isn't handled quite the same way as the other Pages dialogues. You need to manually determine the range. You can do this via a comma separated list. * means all the pages.

So Import Page(s): * from 15 would import all the pages in the document.

You can separate parts of the list using commas. So, the following option means importing pages one and two:

Import Page(s): 1,2 from 15

A hyphen means that you're importing a range from x to y inclusive. So, to import pages 1 and 2

Import Page(s): 1-2 from 15

And to import all pages except page 3 in the document:

Import Page(s): 1-2,4-15 from 15

One very important thing to note is that by default when you're importing a document you don't create the pages. So, you're overwriting the contents of those pages in the document. Toggle the option to create the pages by clicking on the rectangle ☐ Create Page(s) then choose where in the document to insert them in the normal way:

☑ Create Page(s) At End ▼ 4 ⬍

One way that I often use this is if I'm working on a very large document, I have files with different template formats. For example, a chapter file or two column file. Then I import the pages from the document and copy them as many times as necessary.

Obviously you can use Master Pages to get a similar effect which can be quicker, but it's sometimes useful to be able to edit objects on a page.

Guides

We covered Grid Lines above but sometimes you may want to use Guides as well. A Guide is a line on the page that you can use to force some feature into a standard place on the document. For example, say you always want chapter headers to be positioned in the same place on a page. You could create a Guide Line to allow you to accurately position the chapter header.

To manage guides click on Manage Guides... in the Pages menu.

You'll see a list of guides that are separated into directions.

Horizontals (pt)   Verticals (pt)

When you haven't added any guides the list will be empty. To add a guide, click on Add below the type of guide that you want to add. You'll see a little box appear in the list 0.00 pt. Type the distance from either the top or the left margin into the box (depending on whether the guide is vertical or horizontal). Then press enter.

You'll see the guide added to the list:

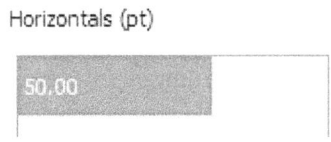

Horizontals (pt)

50.00

You'll also see the guide appear on the page as a red dotted line.

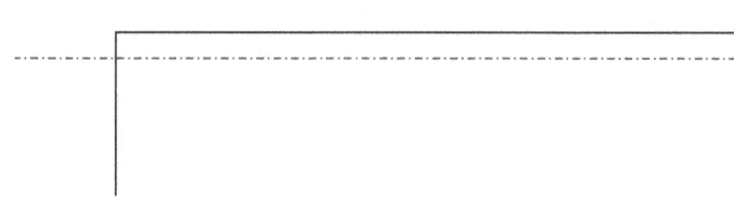

If you want to change the location of a guide double click on it to edit the number.

To delete a guide single click on it, then hit Delete .

By default guides you add only apply to the current page. Apply to All Pages makes the guides you've set for this page also apply to all the other pages in the document.

Column and Row Guides

Columns are a very common feature in lots of documents including Newspapers. They can make it much easier to read a document, and can even increase how efficiently you use paper in your document.

It's possible to add column guidelines very easily from the Column/Row tab. Click onto the tab and you'll see a field for columns (Verticals) and rows (horizontals).

Before you add a column or row it's important to choose the reference point. By default the columns are set equidistant on the page. But if you've got mirrored margins, or margins that are uneven, it can be good to set the reference point to Margins rather than Page so that your columns or rows are based on the actual area that you're going to work on.

Another interesting option is the Selection Feature. Say you're working on a Text Field. You may want the columns to only apply to that text field. Setting the Reference point to Selection will mean that your columns or rows will be based on the width of the actual field you're adding information to.

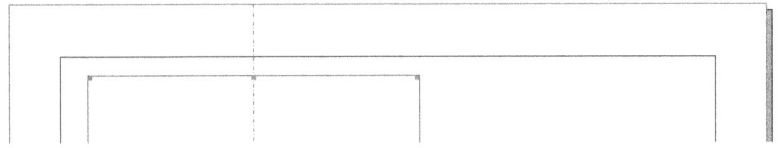

Once you've set the reference point, it's time to add the columns. Change the number field to increase the number of columns or rows.

For example, if we set the vertical we see that our document is divided into two columns:

Finally, it's very common for people to want a gap between the columns. This makes it much easier to read the document. You can add a gap by toggling on ☐ Use Gap: and then entering the width of the gap. For example:

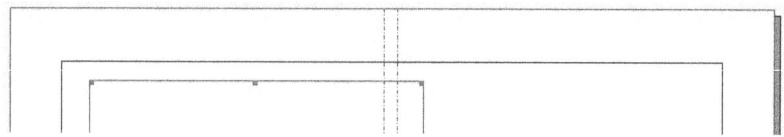

Will result in the following:

Remember that when you set these columns or rows they will generally apply only to the current page unless you click on

Apply to All Pages

Delete All Guides from Current Page or Document

While it's possible to manually delete guides (including columns and rows) from a document it's often quicker to do it automatically. Go to the Misc tab, and then click on to delete guides (this includes columns and rows) from the current page click on:

Delete Guides from Current Page

And to delete guidelines from all the pages of the document click on:

Delete Guides from All Pages

Be careful with these options: it can be difficult to undo them if you're using a document that is very large.

Forcing Objects to Snap to Guides

Just as you can force objects to snap to grid lines it's possible for you to force them to snap to guidelines. Click on

Snap to Guides

in the Pages menu to force inserted objects into grid lines. When you want to turn it off click on

✔ Snap to Guides

again to allow you to insert objects freely.

Page Properties

It's rare to need to change Page Properties from the document default, and in fact this can be problematic – for example if you create a page that is larger than the rest and you want to print it out. But if you click on

Manage Page Properties…

in the Pages menu you'll be able to edit properties.

Most of these properties will be very familiar to you. For example, you can change the size and orientation of the page:

Page Size

Size:	A4 ▼
Orientation:	Portrait ▼
Width: 595.28 pt ⇕	Height: 841.89 pt ⇕

Or you can change Margins so you have custom margins for just the current page:

Margin Guides		
Preset Layouts:	None	▾
Left:	40.00 pt	↕
Right:	40.00 pt	↕
Top:	40.00 pt	↕
Bottom:	40.00 pt	↕
	Printer Margins...	

You can also set the current Master Page for this particular page. I'll go into detail about this in the next section.

Changing the Document Layout via the Arrange Pages Window

When you create a new document you set the Document Layout (for example, single paged or double paged) and it's used throughout the document. It's very rare to change your mind on such a fundamental decision but if you do it's possible to alter this choice in the Arrange Pages Window.

First, click on Arrange Pages in the Windows menu. At the bottom of the window is a Document Layout option. Click on it and you'll see a list of document layouts.

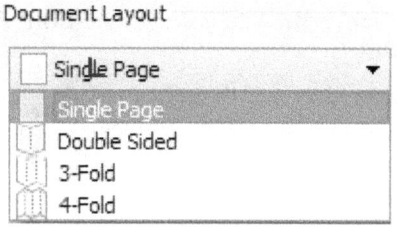

Document Layout

☐ Single Page	▾
Single Page	
Double Sided	
3-Fold	
4-Fold	

When you select the option you'll see that the entire document changes to the new layout.

This can cause problems with the design of the existing pages in your document since things like mirroring may change the position of objects. So review your document carefully after you make such a big change.

8 MASTER PAGE CONCEPTS

You can think of a Master Page as a sort of template containing Guidelines, images and other objects that aren't editable. For example a Master Page used for a company letter might have:

- The Company logo
- A name and address,
- Legal information at the bottom of the page
- Guidelines that are used to place the text frame that will contain the bulk of the letter.

When you apply a Master Page to a Page all the features in the Master Page are added to the page. But the downside to this is that you can't easily edit the content of the Master Page.

Often you'll use the Import Facility where you want to have a template with editable objects (see above).

Converting a Document to a Master Page

Let's say that we've designed a page that we want to use as a master page:

This text belongs to a new master page

L

To store the page as a master page click on

Convert to Master Page... L in Pages.

You'll see a new master page dialogue. Enter the name of the Master Page:

Name: My Master Page|

Assigning a master page to the current page.

Of course, a master page isn't all that useful until you assign it to an existing page. First, make sure you're editing the page which you want to apply the master page to. Then click on

Apply Master Page... L
.

This will bring up the Apply Maaster Pages dialogue. The first step is to choose the Master Page you want to apply.

Master Page: Normal ▼
                My Master Page
                Normal

You can then can decide what pages you want the master page applied to. The default is that it just applies to the current page

● Current Page . If you click on ◯ All Pages the page will apply to all pages in the document, unless you toggle ▢ Within Range on and choose a range.

☑ Within Range 8 ⬍ to 16 ⬍

It's also possible to assign a master page to odd or even pages. I'm going to describe that below. When you're happy and you want to apply the pages click OK .

You'll see that the master page has been applied to the current page (or all pages in the document, or the range that you selected).

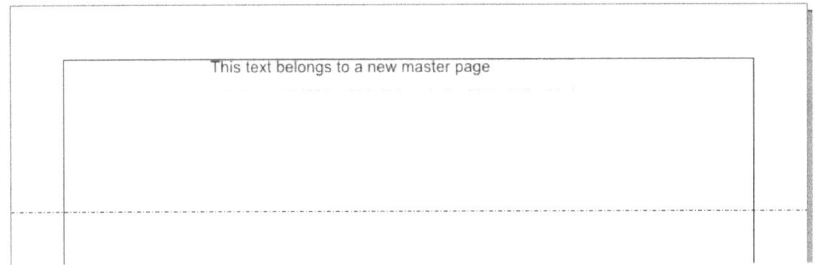

When you try to click the Text Frame "This text belongs to a new master page" you'll find that you can't select or edit it.

Assigning a master page to either odd or even pages

Many times you'll want a different master page on odd and even pages. For example, if you were designing a paperback book you might have a different master page on odd pages – containing your name, and even pages – containing the name of the book.

This is particularly useful when you want to apply mirroring to your book. For example, the page margins on one side of the book may be the reverse of the page margins of the other side.

In fact, applying different master pages to odd and even pages is one of the most common examples of how people use Master Page functionality.

Creating Master Pages for Mirroring

To create a mirror masterpage you need to set the page margins on a specific page. You can do this by going to a blank page and then Manage Page Properties... └ . You'll see that there is the option of setting the Margin Guides in the page properties dialogue.

Margin Guides

Preset Layouts:	None
Left:	80.00 pt
Right:	40.00 pt
Top:	40.00 pt
Bottom:	40.00 pt
	Printer Margins...

I've edited the left margin in this case.

When you click OK you'll see that the margins have changed just for that particular page.

Once you've made any of the other changes (such as adding header text) to the master page, you can create the master page as above saving it with a name like "Right Page".

Applying the Master Page to odd or even pages

Once you've created the Master Page it's pretty easy to apply it to odd or even pages.

Click on Apply Master Page... as above. Choose the Master Page to apply to odd or even pages.

Master Page: Right Master Page ▼

Then click on ○ Even Pages to apply it to all even pages or

○ Odd Pages to apply it to all odd pages. Now, if your document starts on page 1, odd pages will all be left hand pages, and even pages will all be right hand pages. If you start the document on another page it could be the other way round.

Repeat the process (i.e. make the Mirror Master Page for the left hand side if you just created it for the right).

Page Numbers

It's pretty common to include page numbers in headers. When you're editing the Text Frame for your header or footer hover your mouse over character and choose page number to insert an automatic field that displays the current page number for that field, or Number of Pages to display how many pages there are in the document.

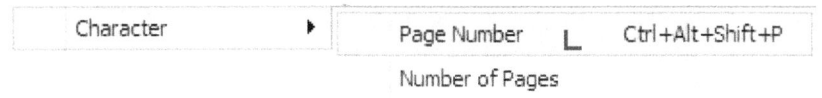

Editing a Master Page

To Edit a master page click on Master Pages... in the edit menu. This will bring up the Master Pages dialogue:

There is a toolbar that allows you to add, delete, and copy master pages. But to Edit a master page simply click on one of the Pages on the List (For example Normal) and the main document view will change to the master page that you're editing. You can then change things on the master page as if it were an ordinary page. But when you close the dialogue by clicking on ▨ all your changes will be applied to any page in your document that is based on that master page.

Delete Master Page

To delete a Master Page click on it in the list of master pages:

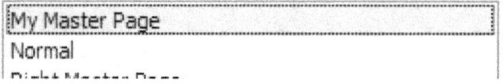

Then click on ▨ . Note that if the master page is being used by any page in the document the delete master page icon will be greyed out. This is because you can only delete master pages that aren't being used.

Copy Master Page

Click on the Master Page to be copied. Then click on Duplicate Master Pages . Type in a name for the new master page Name: Copy #1 of My Master Page and then click OK .

This functionality can be useful if you want to base a master page on another master page. Say, you're making a paperback book. You've got a Blank Right Page that contains only the mirror margins for a right page. Then you want to create a Chapter Right Page which contains guidelines for the Chapter Header, a text frame, and a footer with a page number.

You might also want a normal Content Right Page that contains the header, footer, and content guidelines.

You can create the Blank Right Page first, then use duplicate to copy the margin measurements only editing the features that you want to edit for the master page that you're working on.

Import Master Page

Sometimes you may have set up Master Pages that are useful in another document. To import them click on . Browse for the document by clicking on Select... and using the Open Dialogue to find the file that you want to add.

Once you've chosen the document Scribus will automatically populate the Import Master Pages list. Clicking on it will show all the Master Pages in the document.

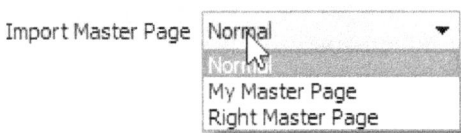

Select the master page that you want to import and click

on 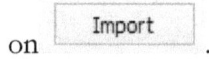 .

When a master page is imported that has the same name as an existing master page Scribus won't have a fit. Instead, it'll just add the phrase Copy X of MASTER PAGE NAME.

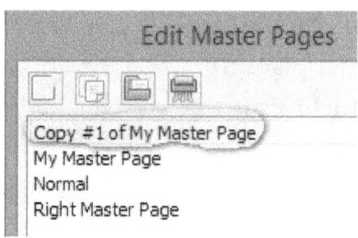

Renaming a master page

If you want to Rename a Master Page double click on it in the Edit Master Pages Dialogue. You'll see a rename Master Page Dialogue:

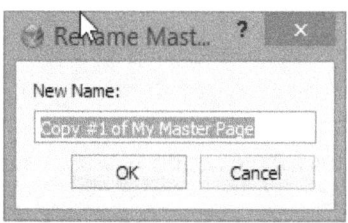

Change the name and then click OK. There is one exception. You can't rename the Master Page called Normal. This is because needs a Master Page Normal which it uses as the default master page whenever you insert a page in the document.

Specifying the Master Page when you insert a page.

While we've already discussed most of the options that you can use when you're inserting a document there is one option that should now make sense. When you insert a page by clicking on 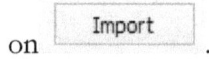 in the Pages menu you'll see one very familiar option:

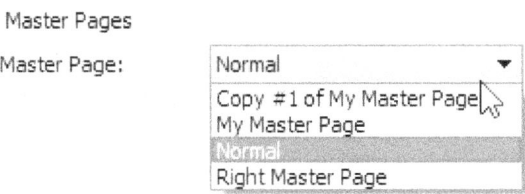

Now that you've seen what a Master Page is, you can tell that by clicking on one of the Master Pages in the document you'll apply that master page to all the pages that you are inserting.

One of the problems with this approach is that it doesn't allow you to apply mirroring. You can get around this by using the Apply Master Page option.

Click on 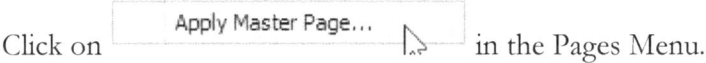 in the Pages Menu.

Choose the master page you want for an odd or even page.

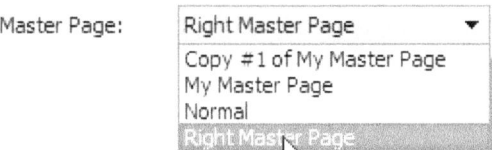

Then whether you want to apply it to Even or Odd pages

Finally click the rectangle  and choose insert range to match the pages you just inserted. (E.g. if you inserted pages 4 to 6)

Repeat the steps to apply the master page for the other page in your range. Admittedly this is quite fiddly but it's not often that you'll apply these kind of options more than a few times in a document. Normally since you've made the material elsewhere (in a word processor or text editor and a photo editor or illustrator) you'll be working on the layout close to the end of a project which has already been completed

.

9 TABLES

So far we've worked on some basic objects. We've created text frames which contain Text, and also Image Frames that can contain pictures. But there are several more types of objects that can be very useful.

Since childhood you'll have regularly come across one of these commonly used objects – the Table. A table is used to display large amounts of data.

Now, in theory it's possible to make Tables using Scribus. You can insert a table by clicking on Insert Table in the Insert Menu.

Then you draw the Table Frame in the normal way.

When you let go Scribus will prompt you for the number of rows and columns.

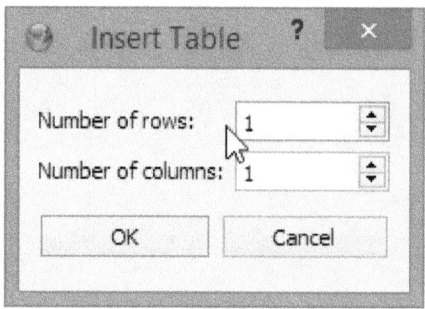

Enter the number, and you'll see something that looks a lot like a table appear on the document.

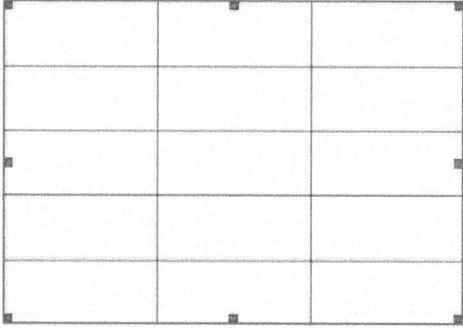

Maybe that sounds a bit sarcastic, but the reality is that the Table is a definite pain to work with. It's just a collection of text frames that have all been grouped together. This means that:

- To change the size of the cells you have to do it individually.
- To add content you have to ungroup the cells first.
- In fact, the whole thing is pretty unwieldy.

In the same way that I wouldn't create the text in a document by typing directly into the Story Editor (even though in theory you could do so) I wouldn't create a Table in my document using Scribus.

Instead, I'd create a table in another program and then import it into Scribus.

Unfortunately, this is a little harder than importing text.

Getting a table from LibreOffice Calc into Scribus

One free program that you can use to create the table is LibreOffice Calc. I've written a detailed book on how to use it (Use LibreOffice Calc) but the basics aren't too complicated to understand. Once you've installed the software and opened a file you can type the data in pretty easily.

For example I create the following table in LibreOffice Calc:

E10		✓	f_x Σ =		
	A	B	C	D	
1					
2					
3		Number Of Protagonists Vs Dragons			
4			Superman	The Hobbit	
5		Protagonists	1	1	
6		Dragons	0	1	
7					
8					
9					

And I want to insert it into my document. The tricky thing is that once you have the table you need to find a way to turn it into an image. You can do this pretty easy using Print Screen (the prt scr key on the keyboard) on windows. Press Print Screen to copy the screen to the clipboard. Open Paint and paste the clipboard into the window by going to the Home tab and clicking:

Paste
▼

Then make sure that you're in select mode:

Draw a rectangle round the image. (Click and hold the mouse at one corner of the rectangle and move the mouse to the other corner). When you're happy let go:

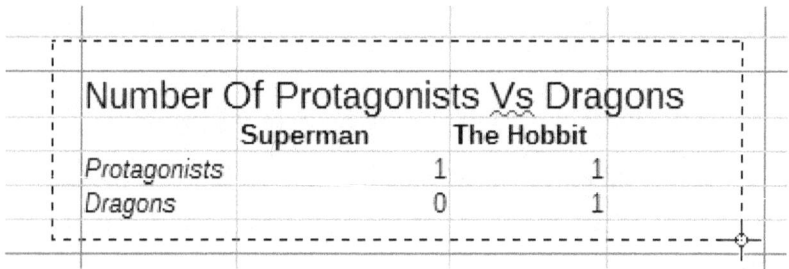

Then Press ⊠ Crop . You'll see that you've removed all the extraneous detail from the table.

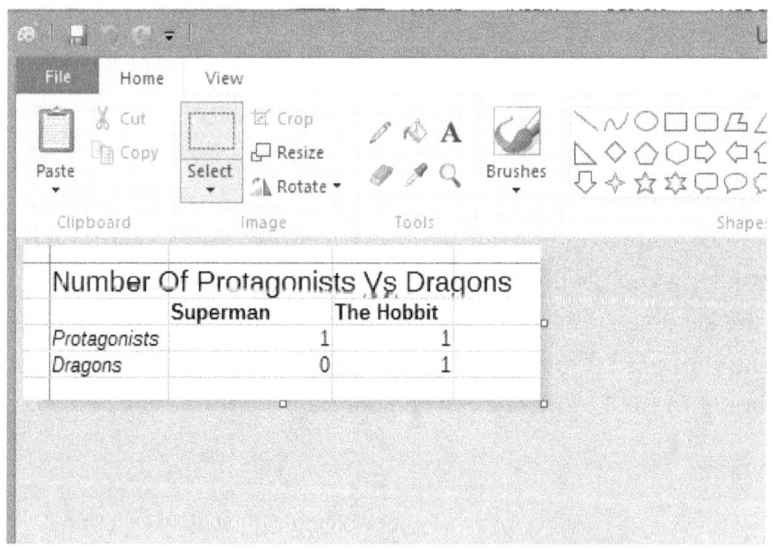

To save the Image that you've edited, click 🔲 File

then then use the Save As dialogue in the normal way.

Once you have created an image it's easy to insert it into the document. Just follow the steps in the Image Tutorial above.

Obviously, you can adjust the spreadsheet to remove columns, add borders, or change the font sizes if you want to. And you can use whatever spreadsheet program you want to make the tables. It's just that LibreOffice is free but if you've got one that you prefer that's fine.

Note that you can use screenshots to produce image of the screen on all major platforms. The details will differ slightly depending on the platform but a quick google will tell you how to do it in your platform.

Actually, these steps are quite powerful because you can also create charts of all kinds using the spreadsheet program of your choice and then insert them into your document in the same way.

10 SHAPES

Intuitively everyone knows what you mean when you talk about inserting shapes into an object. They're things like squares, circles, arrows, and special shapes like jigsaw pieces and stars. The main purpose of these shapes is to make the document look more appealing. Although they can be used in slightly more complicated ways as well.

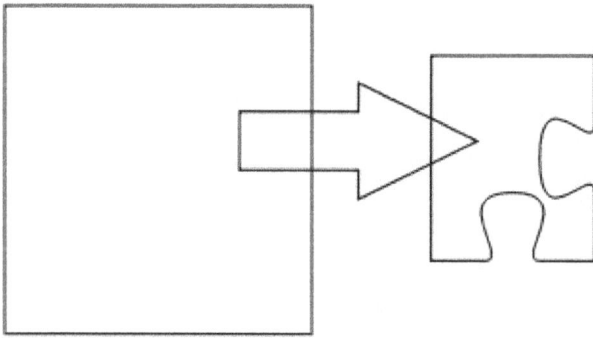

For example, you can use it to highlight a column title in a piece of text:

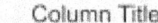

Column Title

This is a column of text. You
can use shapes to add interest
to it.

As you work more and more with Scribus you'll start to use
shapes more frequently for all kinds of things.

Shapes can be used to join multiple objects together, to highlight
part of an object, or just to add visual interest to your document. You
can fill shapes, change the outlines, and group them together.

Inserting a Shape

If you hover your mouse over insert shape in the Insert menu
you'll see lots of different Shape categories. For example Default
shapes, such as rectangles and circles, Arrows, Flow Chart Shapes,
Jigsaw and Special Shapes.

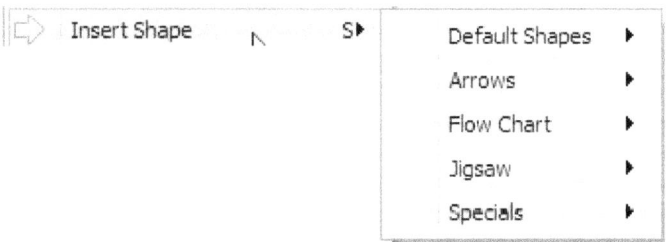

Hover your mouse over one of these categories and you'll see
the items in the category. Click on one of the items to select it to
insert.

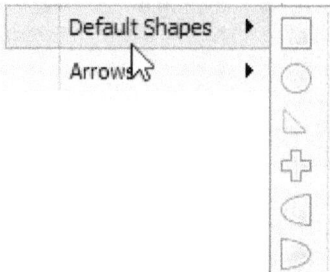

Obviously there are a lot of these shapes in each category, but after hunting around a bit I'm sure you'll find the shape that you want to insert. Once you've clicked on the shape that you want to insert actually putting it in the document works just like any other Frame. Click on one corner, hold the mouse down, and move to the opposite corner.

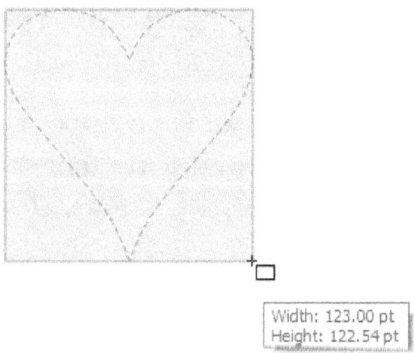

When you let go the shape will be added to the document.

You can then Move the shape in the same way as any other Frame (by clicking and holding on the shape then moving the mouse to where you want the image to go.)

Resize it by clicking on the shape and using the rectangles in the same way as an Image Frame

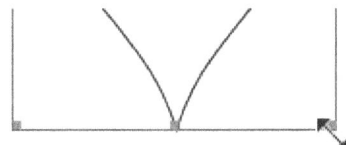

Or even delete it by clicking on it and pressing the delete key at the top right hand side of your keyboard. In other words, for most purposes once you've inserted a shape it acts pretty much the same way as an image.

Changing Objects Colour

Sometimes you don't want just a blank colour in your shape. Fortunately it's pretty easy to give a shape or any object colour.

First, right click on the object. If the Properties Dockable Window doesn't open automatically, click on

Properties   F2   to open it.

To change the colours of any object click

on Colours .

Line colour

To set the Line Colour click on . Then double click on the

colour that you want to use for the line around the object.

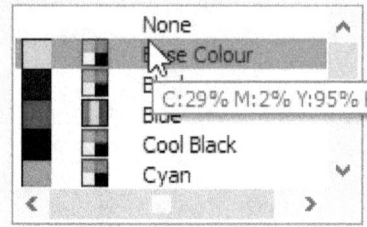

If you click on None the border around the object will be clear.

Fill Colour

Click on  to change the fill colour. As above you'll see a list of colours and you can choose one.

In the following example I used None for the Line colour and Red for the Fill colour.

Both line and fill colour have a shade option. By default it is at 100. If you reduce the percentage the shape will become a lighter shade

This can be worth experimenting with if the original shade has too much colour or is too forceful for your use.

Types of Fill

When you're working with fill colours especially it's worth realising that Scribus allows you to fill the colour with MORE than just a single shade of colour. You can fill the shape with Patterns and gradients of all kinds by clicking on the combo box just above the list of colours.

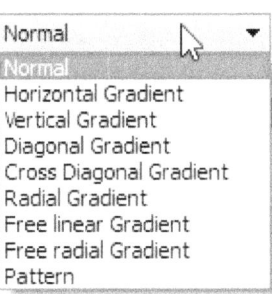

Opaqueness

One thing that people often don't realise is that with all Frames and Objects you have a lot of control over how strongly the object on top hides the content of the object beneath it. While by default shapes are set to cover over an object, you can make them see through.

For example, take the following combination of text:

If in the Colours section above you change the Opacity to half:

You'll see that the heart becomes partially see through.

Please insert a romantic poem here
It doesn't come into my mind,
I'd like to send it to you right now,
But this is lame,
I bought a book of poems then,
realized you'd read them all.
I'm sorry but my poetry is
Not as good as theirs at all

Of course you can vary the shade and the opacity by taste. Everyone likes slightly different versions.

Using the colour wheel

In the above examples we chose colours based on the document pallet. But sometimes you may want to add a colour to the pallet. The colour wheel allows you to do this. Click on Colour Wheel... in the Extras window.

You'll see a dialogue with a large colour wheel. Note that the centre of the wheel contains the colour that you're currently over. You can move around the wheel to get different colours. Click on the wheel at the place where you have the colour that you want to use.

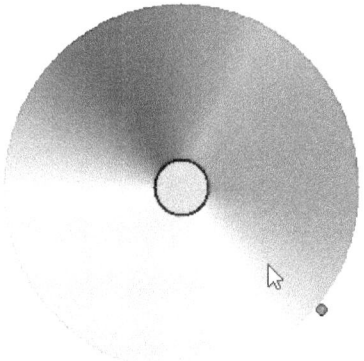

For this purpose I suggest clicking on Merge to add the choices you've made to the colour wheel.

11 POLYGON

I don't use Polygons often in the documents that I make but Scribus does offer it if you need it. To insert a polygon hover your mouse over Insert Polygon in the Insert menu then click on properties.

The default polygon that Scribus inserts is a 4 sided regular polygon. Also known as a "square". There's a preview window of the current polygon on the right hand side of the dialogue.

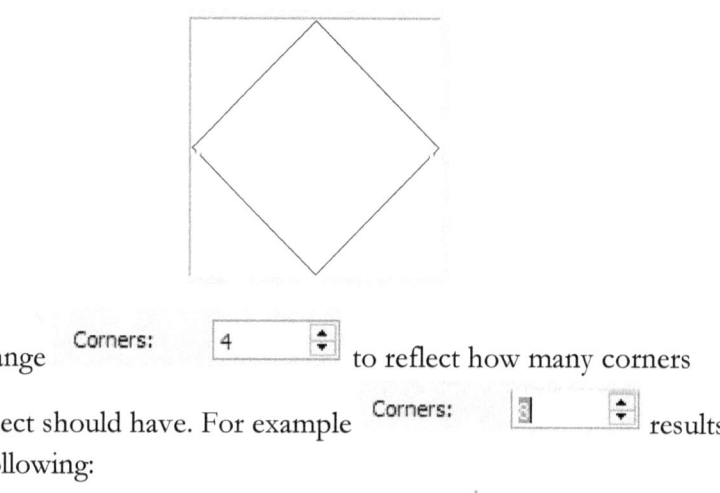

Change Corners: 4 to reflect how many corners your object should have. For example Corners: 3 results in the following:

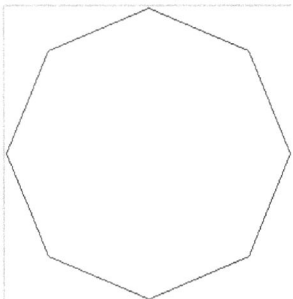

The preview window shows the default angle of the polygon. You can slide the bar up or down to rotate it around the central point. It's worth experimenting while watching what happens in the preview window.

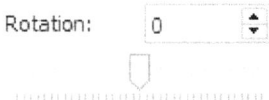

In addition to this you can toggle on 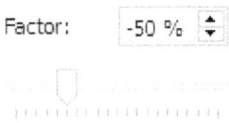 by clicking on the rectangle in order to change the Factor. You can slide the bar over so the factor is concave or convex. For example apply the following settings to the default square:

You'll see that it becomes a very different shape!

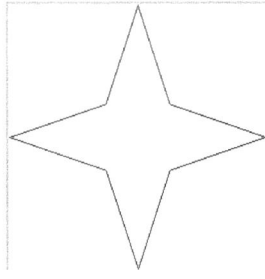

Finally, you can give a polygon greater curvature. For example sliding the bar across to 40%

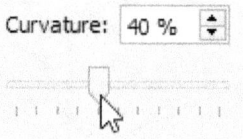

Will give you a curved star:

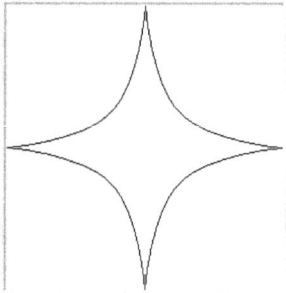

When you're happy with the polygon click OK and then draw the shape onto the document like any other shape.

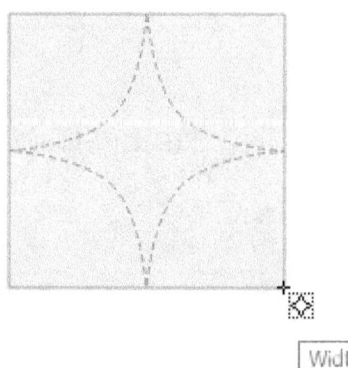

12 LINES AND CURVES

Lines and curves are very common feature in a lot of documents. Scribus allows you to have lots of different types of lines. These include the ability to have dots, dashes, and even arrow heads. But the settings to do this aren't completely obvious.

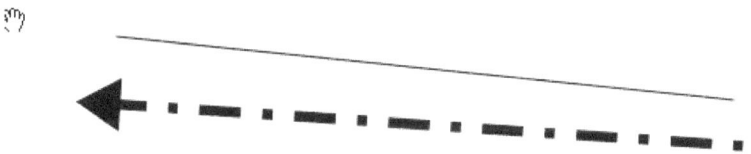

To insert a line click on 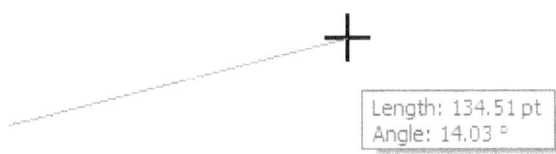 in the Insert Menu. You can draw the line onto the canvas like any other shape, clicking and holding the mouse at one end then moving the mouse to the other and letting go.

When you let go you'll see the line on the document. The basic line looks pretty much like what you'd expect:

To change the width, the end, and even the type of line right click on it and then 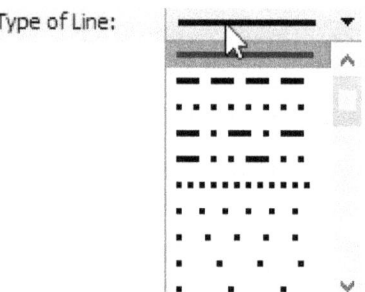. Click on Line in the properties dialogue. The first major way to change the line is to select the type of line box. Once you've clicked on it the function of this box is pretty obvious. You can see a list of different line types – which is basically various types of dots and dashes.

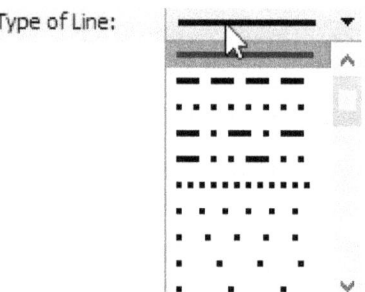

I also regularly use the start arrow and end arrow. Once you click on it you'll see a range of shapes although I often just use the first couple – which produce good "standard" arrow heads that are very much multipurpose.

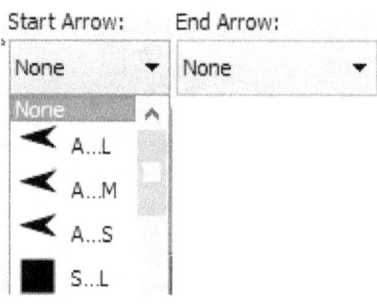

The final option that I use often with lines is the Line Width option. Type in the width that you want the line to have. For example, 5 pt Is a thick line.

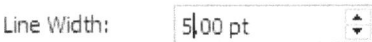

When you click out of the Line Width field you'll see the line change to a much greater width:

Note that you can resize a line by clicking at the corner. Red circles appear at each end. Click on the circle and hold the mouse down then move the mouse to the place on the document that you want the line to end.

Freehand Line

The above lines are very useful but they are all straight lines. And sometimes you just have to draw a wriggly line. You can do this by clicking ![Insert Freehand Line F] in the Insert menu. As you move the mouse to the document you'll see it change to ![pen] . When you click and hold you'll notice the line is drawn anywhere on the document you go until you let go of the mouse.

You can draw the line in any shape you want. When you let go it'll appear on the document. You can resize and move the line like any other shape – by clicking on it. You can also change the line thickness and type, and even add an arrow to it just like a straight line.

Bezier Curve

Sometimes you don't want a hand drawn line, or a straight line. You want a curved line. You can do this by clicking on

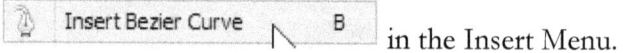 in the Insert Menu.

It can be tricky to understand how to use these curved lines. It's important to remember that you're doing two things:

1. Drawing the line and,
2. Setting the curve.

Drawing the line is relatively straight forward. Simply click on the document where you want the line to begin, then move the mouse to where you want the line to end. Click again to fix the line, then move the mouse to the next location. Keep on clicking until you're happy with the line you've drawn.

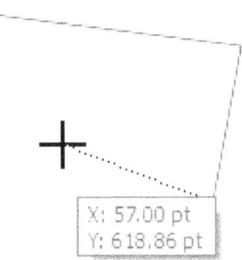

Then right click to draw the line.

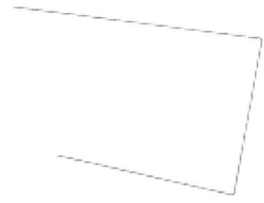

Note that you can set line properties for this type of curve in the same way that you can with ordinary lines. But there's something missing in these instructions so far – setting the curve.

Curves are composed of nodes – which are the edges of the lines, and control points which dictate what direction the line should be shaped towards. So you've edited the nodes and if you want the curve to actually be a curve you'll want to edit the control points too.

When you click on the curve to start it, instead of letting go keep holding the mouse. You're now editing a control point. If you move the mouse you'll see that the node (i.e. the end of the line you've drawn so far) remains in the same place. But the control point moves.

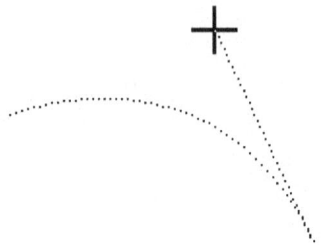

When you let go you'll start editing the next node. I.e. you'll be drawing a new line. You just move the mouse to the end of the next line, click (or click and hold to edit the control point) and repeat the process. When you've drawn the entire shape that you want to draw right click. This inserts the shape.

You can boils up very complicated shapes this way.

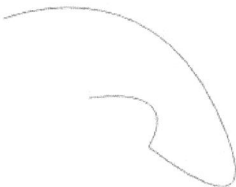

Look at the drawing of the control point above. What you're controlling is the angle of the curve as it approaches the node. These types of curves always want to be smooth, so as you move the mouse around the screen you'll get all sorts shapes.

One thing that can get confusing is that the line will try to carry on with the curve that you just made. I.e. the curve as you leave a node will be the starting angle for the next node.

Wow, that's a bit of a mouthful. But you can see what I mean as I edit the node below. Because the line already has an angle associated with it, Scribus is drawing a curve that matches the angle from the existing line.

This is tricky to get used to. But once you understand the theory – that the curve is already moving in a certain direction and Scribus is just trying to smooth it as much as possible in a parabola – it makes it pretty easy to make some very complicated shapes.

All of the above is something that you'll need to practice a certain amount. It doesn't come easy for everyone so don't get too frustrated if you have a few problems.

13 EDITING SHAPES AND CONTOUR LINES

The following Bezier curve doesn't look much like one. I made a mistake when I added it. I forgot to alter the control point.

You can fix these kinds of errors by opening the properties windows (right click on the shape) and

selecting Properties F2) then clicking

on Shape .

The first thin in the Shapes tab is an Edit button. Click on it.

Shape: Edit...

You'll see quite a complicated dialogue window with all sorts of buttons. It's pretty scary when you look at it for the first time. On the document you'll see your curve. It's got blue points and pink points. The blue points are the nodes. The pink points are the control points.

Editing Nodes.

The first thing I'm going to do is edit a node. You can add a new node by clicking on  and then going to the point in the line or the curve that you want to add the node and clicking on it.

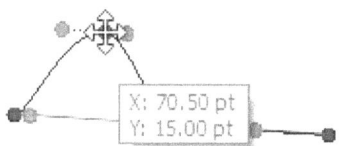

Note that just adding the new node also adds new control points. These control points allow you to alter the curve of the line.

To Move a node click on  and then click on the node. Hold the mouse button down then drag it to the location in the document you want it to go.

X: 70.50 pt
Y: 15.00 pt

Let go of the mouse when you're happy with the position. Note that because you moved the node the control points will also move. You can see how they work more clearly on the picture below.

You can delete a node by clicking on and then the node. If you make a mistake while editing

Editing Control Points

Basically, editing control points works the same way as editing nodes. You can't add new control points except by adding a node but you can move them by using the options provided. But before I tell you how to move the control points I'm going to explain how to reset them – in case you make an error. Resetting a Control point means putting the control point at the same place as a node. While you are in the mode for moving nodes click on a node to select it:

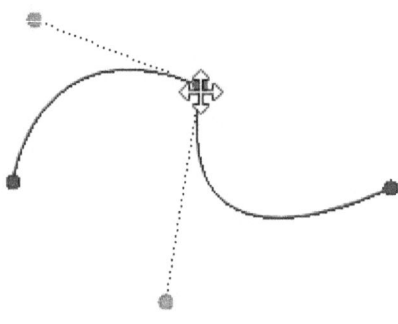

Then click on the Reset icon .

Now that you can reset the control points it's time to move them. There are several options for moving a control point. The first option is to move each point individually. I think that's probably the most commonly chosen option. The second option is to move both points symmetrically.

Click on ![icon] to start moving the control points. Then ![icon] to move them symmetrically. Move the control point. Note that since both control points will move towards the mouse pointer the curve is symmetrical when the pointer is in the centre of the line

If it's not in the centre the curve won't be symmetrical but the control points will both move to where the mouse pointer is:

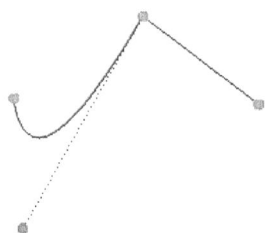

The other choice is to move each control point separately. Make sure you are in Control Point editing mode ![icon] and then click on move individually ![icon] . Click on the control point that you want to move and drag is across to the new location.

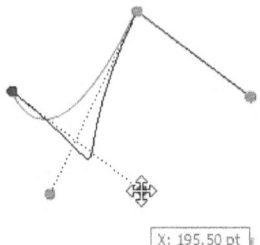

You can reset an individual control point by clicking on it and then clicking on ![icon] .

All of this may seem quite complicated but as you try it out you find out quickly how powerful it is. You can use this to manipulate the text around an invisible object, control the space around a picture, or just make funky looking lines.

Sheering the Path

These commands allow you to tilt the shape to the left or right. For example, take this shape.

You can sheer nodes to the left or right.

Sheer central node to the left ![icon]   Then sheer to the right ![icon] :

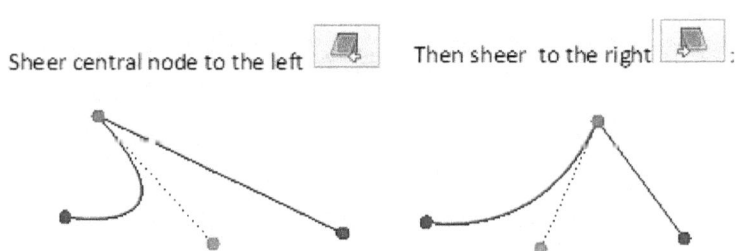

And you can sheen nodes up or down:

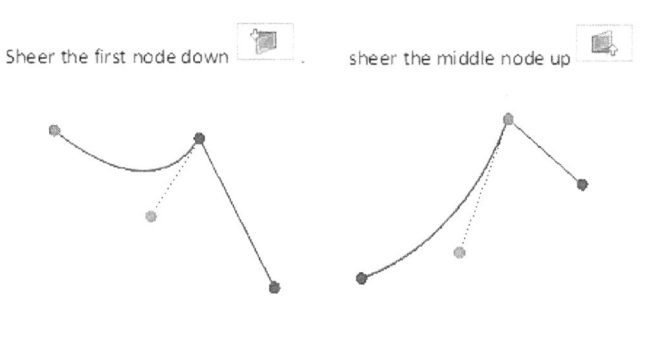

Sheer the first node down   .   sheer the middle node up

:

Mirror the Path

Mirroring the path is another way of saying that you're flipping the drawing around horizontally or vertically. Make sure you're editing the properties of the drawing. For example, this one:

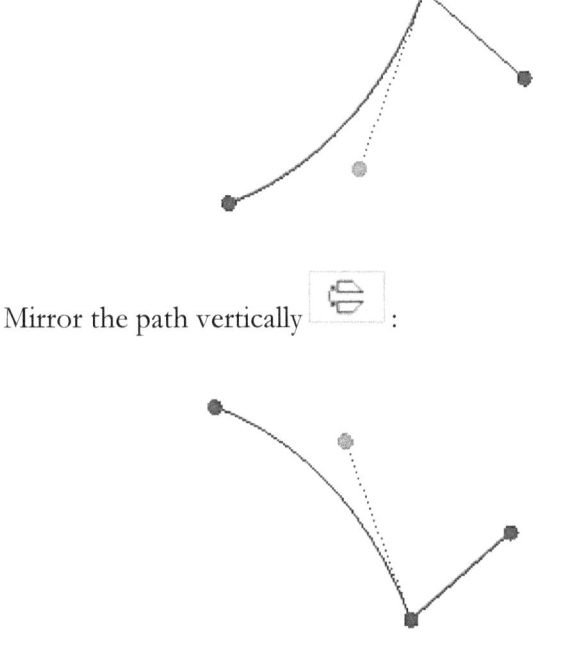

Mirror the path vertically   :

Mirror the path horizontally

Rotating the Path

You can rotate the image counter-clockwise by clicking [icon] or clockwise by clicking [icon] . By the icons to rotate it is a text box which controls how many degrees the image is rotated each time you click the button [1 °] .

Shrink and Enlarge

I've already shown you this, but to remind you it's possible to shrink [icon] or enlarge [icon] the size of the path by the amount chosen in the text box, either as an absolute value or a percentage.

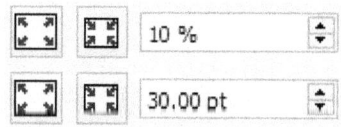

Contour Lines

We've already seen the main use of the contour line. When you

Use Contour Line in the Shapes Menu Text is wrapped around the contour of the image.

When you edit a shape like a polygon sometimes the contour doesn't get updated immediately. In which case, text will not wrap correctly. To solve this you will have to edit the contour line. You might also edit the contour line if you want to add space around an object or shape.

You can edit the contour line via **Edit...** , and then clicking on the rectangle by **Edit Contour Line** . If the contour line is incorrect after you've edited the shape of an object, the quickest solution is to click **Reset Contour Line** .

Note that editing the contour line works just the same way as editing a normal line. There are nodes (in blue) and control points (in pink) that you move in just the same way as editing a normal line. The contour line itself is blue. Most often you'll just use the expand features to create a border around the image.

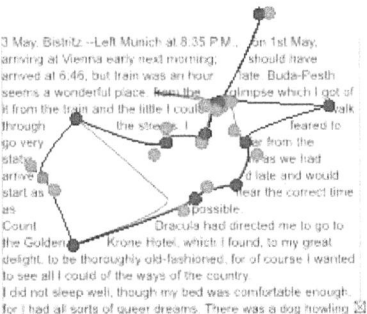

Once you finish editing click on the rectangle by **Edit Contour Line** again. The contour line will disappear (except for a faint grey line) and you can see how text wraps around the new contours.

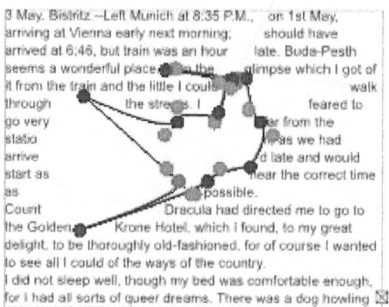

This can cause an interesting effect if you change the line colour to nothing. You see the effect best when you do a print preview or by turning on preview mode in the View menu. It's a bit like a cut out in the text:

3 May. Bistritz.--Left Munich at 8:35 P.M.,   on 1st May, arriving at Vienna early next morning; should have   arrived at 6:46, but train was an hour late. Buda-Pesth seems a   wonderful place, from the glimpse which I got of it from the train   and the little I could walk through the streets. I feared to go very far   from the station, as   we had arrived   late and would start as near   the correct time as possible. Count   Dracula had directed me to go to go to   the Golden Krone Hotel, which I   found, to my great delight, to be thorough   ly old-fashioned, for of course I wanted to see all I   could of the ways of the country. I did not   sleep well, though my bed was comfortable enough, for I had all sorts of queer dreams. There was a dog howling all night under my window, w wildest and leasimaginative whirlpool; if so my stay may be very interesting. (Mem., I must ask the Count all about them.)

14 TYPESETTING WORK

Many of the typesetting tasks such as kernelling and hyphenation are automatically handled by Scribus. Further typesetting choices are in effect handled through the style and font choices that you make. But in addition to these automatic functions it's possible to make a huge range of typesetting choices while working within Scribus.

In this tutorial we're going to learn some of these features.

Inserting Glyphs

A document is generally made up of basic letters and numbers from the host language (most likely, English) but there are often characters such as the copyright sign ©that aren't used often but are sometimes necessary. These special characters can seem to be difficult to insert.

To insert a Glyph into your document, click on Glyph... ⌐ .

Then click on . You'll see an entire character set that you can scroll down through to find the character that you want. Only characters available for the current font will be shown.

When you click on one of the symbols you'll see that it's added to the list of Glyphs to Insert.

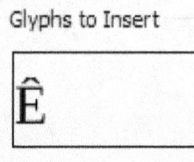

You can't edit the list directly. Instead you have to click on Clear if you change your mind. Note that you can change the font Font: Tr Liberation Serif Regular ▾ for example to wingdings if you want to use symbols that aren't available in the current font.

For people with a lot of experience at desk top publishing there's an option to type the correct character code into the box provided. For example type Insert Code: 01aa| and press enter in the above font and you see a new glyph to insert:

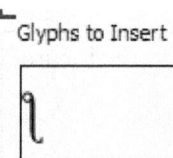

When you're happy with the Glyphs that you are inserting you can click Insert .

In theory it's possible to load character pallets from files, or search through a list of values. I've got to admit that I don't recommend these features because I find that many people have difficulty getting them to work. I prefer to insert Glyphs as above.

Inserting Special Characters

In addition to the above method of inserting all kinds of characters into a document there is also the ability to add all kinds of special characters to a document. We've already seen one of them above where we included a page number.

Page Number and Number of Pages

To insert the Page Number or the Number of Pages hover your mouse over Character in the Insert menu and click on these choices.

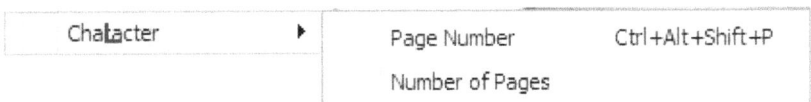

For example, I added this to the top of my

Page 1 or 14

document: . As you change your document you'll see that the values on both types of special characters can change. For example were you insert or delete a page. Scribus automatically updates these fields so that you don't need to worry about it. If the field hasn't updated deselect the text field then click on it again to select it. You should see the field update itself automatically.

Inserting Legal characters

You can insert a copyright symbol by hovering your mouse over Character in the Insert menu and clicking

on Copyright . You'll see the copyright

symbol in your document: ©

In exactly the same way hover your mouse over Character in the insert menu to find options for Registered Trademark and Trademark.

Registered Trademark

Trademark

Inserting Solidus (slash), Bullet, and Middle Dot

Bullets are useful when you're producing a list of points. Middle Dots aren't used as frequently in English although they can be a symbol used in mathematics (another way of specifying product). All three of these options can be found by hovering your mouse over Character in the Insert Menu.

Solidus

Bullet

Middle Dot

Inserting various forms of dash or hyphen

In all honesty Scribus takes a lot of the typesetting work involved in Hyphenating words (see below) but that doesn't mean it isn't possible to do it manually. You can insert em- and en- dashes, hyphens, and even non-breaking hyphens (the difference between a breaking character and a non-breaking one is that a breaking hyphen doesn't force the word onto the next line, i.e. you can split the word into two while justifying or aligning it. Whereas, with a non-breaking hyphen the word has to be treated as one unit.)

All the following options are available by hovering your mouse over Character in the Insert menu.

One of the most interest features is inserting Soft Hyphen. This is an optional hyphen that you use when there is too large a gap between words on the next line. Where a word would otherwise be shifted to the next line, for example:

posuere eget, la

Adding a soft hyphen means that part of the word is retained above the line:

Donec metus massa, mollis vel, tempus placerat, vestibulum condimentum, ligula. Nunc lacus metus, p-
osuere eget, lacinia eu, varius quis, libero. Aliquam nonummy adipiscing augue.

Note though that soft hyphens only force hyphenation where the word is otherwise forced onto the next line. So, adding a soft hyphen to a word in the middle of the line won't make any difference. The purpose of soft hyphens is to prevent really awkward typesetting where there are huge gaps between words when the document is justified.

Soft Hyphen	Ctrl+Shift+-
Non Breaking Dash	Ctrl+Alt+-

A non-breaking dash prevents a line break directly after the dash. So the word stays together.

There are several other options, such as inserting an Em Dash, En Dash, Figure Dash or Quotation Dash that you can access by hovering your mouse over Character in the Insert menu. These pretty much work as you'd probably expect them to work.

Em Dash

En Dash

Figure Dash

Quotation Dash

Inserting Quotes

Hover your mouse over Quote in the Insert menu to see a long list of quotes that you can insert into the document. As a general rule I suggest restraining yourself to the main single, double and apostrophe quotes unless there is a very good reason to do otherwise.

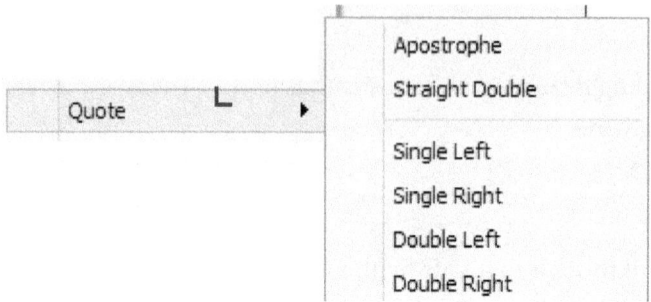

But there are a lot of other quotation methods that you can use if they are appropriate to the task at hand.

Inserting Spaces

The automatic justification and hyphenation that Scribus performs is generally highly effective. It produces very nice results. Professional typesetters may wish to adjust this automatic spacing. They can by hovering their mouse over Spaces & Breaks in the Insert menu.

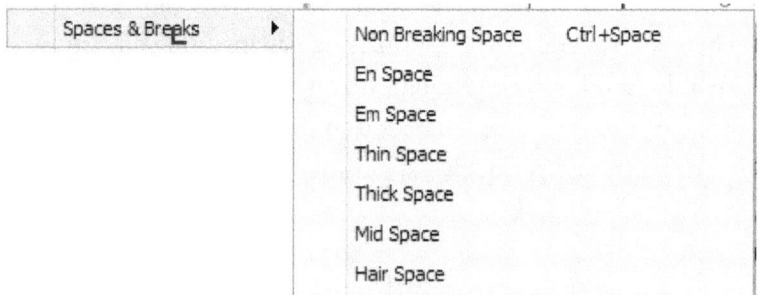

You'll also notice a special space, called a Zero Width Space. This option is right at the bottom. It's an invisible space that is used to keep words together on the same line.

Zero Width Space

There are quite a range of different sized spaces that you can use. I'm sure that as you experiment with them you'll notice that you can use them to fine tune the way that Scribus typesets work with a great deal of accuracy.

One important use of the Non Breaking spaces is that they can keep words together – like a proper name – where you don't want a visible mark like a hyphen between them.

Inserting Breaks

You'll probably often find that you're inserting breaks into the document.

A new line break is obvious, it's what happens when you press enter. I.e. you're shifted to a new line. A Frame Break will shift the rest of the text to the next linked frame. A column break will shift the text to the next column.

You can access these commands by hovering your mouse over Spaces & Breaks in the Insert menu.

New Line	Shift+Return
Frame Break	Ctrl+Return
Column Break	Ctrl+Shift+Return

Inserting Ligatures

I don't often use Ligatures myself since I think that they are old fashioned. Scribus does support them. Hover your mouse over Ligature in the Insert menu and then insert the ligature that you want.

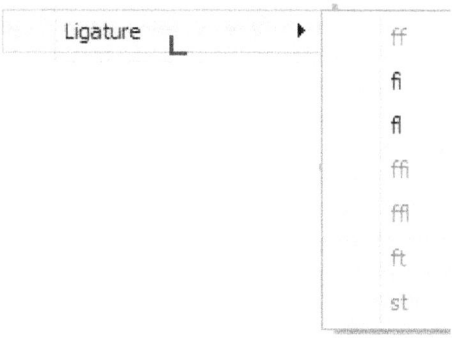

Note that the difference between using Ligatures and not is fairly subtle (first without, second with flair flair) but it does make a little bit of a difference in the document.

Automatically Hyphenate Words

In the old days Hyphenating words was a very time consuming and expensive process. Now, it's fairly simple because Scribus automates most of the choices for you. Click

Hyphenate Text in the Extras menu to automatically hyphenate text:

urpis egestas. Proin phare-

I find that Scribus does a very good job of this without requiring much manual intervention. Although it is possible to intervene using Non Breaking characters as above.

Dehyphenate Words

When you're importing words into a text frame from another document sometimes someone will have already typeset a section of the text or will simply attempt to typeset words themselves. When this happens you can be left with large amounts of text where the hyphenation is simply wrong.

To remove hyphens from a text frame select the text frame, then click Dehyphenate Text in the Extras menu.

Replace quotes with Smart Quotes

Sometimes when importing text into a text frame you'll find that you're using simple quotations. But often you'll want to change these quotation marks to a standard format such as smart quotes (curly quotes that curve into the text), or other forms of quotes.

Scribus allows you to do this automatically with the Autoquote and Autoquote2 script in the Scripts window.

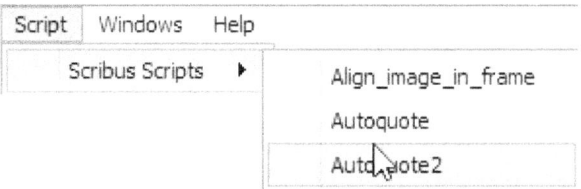

The steps to run these scripts are pretty self-explanatory. For example with autoquote first select the language (en is English):

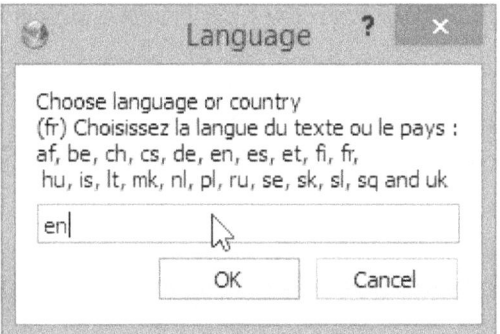

Then follow the dialogue instructions. The first screen asks if you want spaces inside the quotes, and whether to apply it to existing spaces (for this question I'd suggest that since it's better to keep the document consistent it's also as a general rule better to say yes to this question.

When you've run the script it will tell you how many spaces you've replaced.

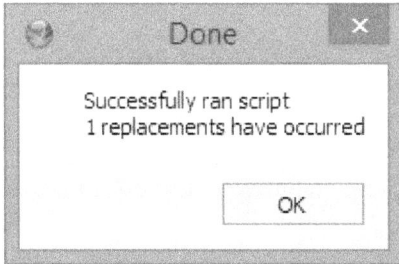

It can be useful to experiment using a trial run before using these scripts. You can do this by saving a backup version first.

Text Properties

So far we've already described some of the Text Properties but there is quite a bit to cover. It's important to remember that Scribus has been designed to be a fully professional DTP suite that can be used for almost any DTP problem.

Remember right click on the Text Frame then click

Properties   F2   to show the Frame Properties. These Properties affect only the content of the current Frame. The document as a whole is not affected.

Click on the Text in the Properties window in order to set the Text Properties for that particular frame.

There are some default settings that you are probably already aware of. For example the Font and Font Effect (i.e. normal or Regular, Bold, Italic).

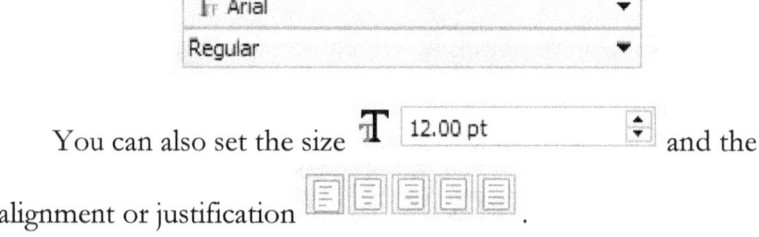

You can also set the size **T** 12.00 pt and the alignment or justification .

One default field that you haven't seen it is the Linespacing field. This field allows you to determine the space between one line in a document and the next line.

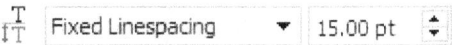

When you click onto the Linespacing you can see the option to set Linespacing automatically. Scribus does quite a good job of making the document as aesthetically pleasing as possible when it does Automatic Linespacing so this is an option you might want to try out.

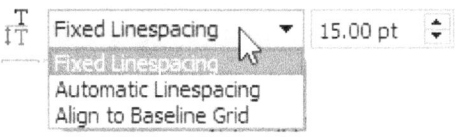

Baseline Grid

One of the most interesting settings in this group is the Align to Baseline Grid setting. We haven't seen the Baseline Grid so far but it solves a problem you might see during editing large documents. Because each frame can start in different positions in the page the text in your document won't always line up between frames.

3 May. Bistritz.--Left Munich at 8:35 P.M., on 1st May, arriving at Vienna early next morning; should have arrived at 6:46, but train was an hour late. Buda-Pesth seems a wonderful place, from the glimpse which I got of it from the

3 May. Bistritz.--Left Munich at 8:35 P.M., on 1st May, arriving at Vienna early next morning; should have arrived at 6:46, but train was an hour late. Buda-Pesth seems a wonderful place, from the glimpse

The Baseline Grid is rather like other Grids that we've seen in the document, only it looks a bit like the rules notepaper you might have used in school when you were learning to write.

To turn it on, click on Show Baseline Grid in the view menu:

3 May. Bistritz.--Left Munich at 8:35 P.M., on 1st May, arriving at Vienna early next morning; should have arrived at 6:46, but train was an hour late. Buda-Pesth seems a wonderful place, from the glimpse which I got of it from the ⊠

3 May. Bistritz.--Left Munich at 8:35 P.M., on 1st May, arriving at Vienna early next morning; should have arrived at 6:46, but train was an hour late. Buda-Pesth seems a wonderful place, from the glimpse ⊠

Once you've set both frames to align to the baseline grid you'll see that they line up with each other even though they start in slightly different places on the page.

3 May. Bistritz.--Left Munich at 8:35 P.M., on 1st May, arriving at Vienna early next morning; should have arrived at 6:46, but train was an hour late. Buda-Pesth seems a wonderful place, from the glimpse which I got of it from the

3 May. Bistritz.--Left Munich at 8:35 P.M., on 1st May, arriving at Vienna early next morning; should have arrived at 6:46, but train was an hour late. Buda-Pesth seems a wonderful ⊠place, from the glimpse ⊠

Colour and Effects

The Colour and Effects properties give you access to a larger range of effects. The first set of choices are the text colour. When setting these properties if you have selected the Frame it will affect all the text in the frame, but if you select (i.e. highlight with the mouse) a portion of the text it will only affect that text.

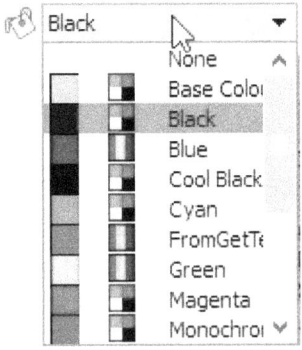

Remember also that you can add colours to the default list through the colour wheel.

There's a shade option to the right of the colour. Once you click on it you can set the shade of the colour.

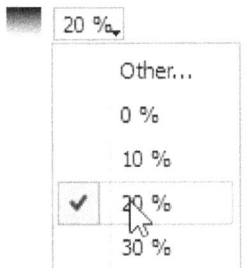

The first box is black at 100%, the second is black at 50%:

3 May. Bistritz.--Left Munich   3 May. Bistritz.--Left
at 8:35 P.M., on 1st May,   Munich at 8:35 P.M., on
arriving at Vienna early next   1st May, arriving at

Below the colour options are a lot of other effect options. Some of these you've seen before such as underline ⨃ although you can also underline each word individually using 🆆:

⎺⎺ ⏀.⎼⎼.⎽ ⎺.. ⎼⎽⎺ ⎼⎽⎼,

ng at Vienna early ne

⎼⎼⎼. ⎽⎼⎺⎒⎺⎺ ⎼⎺⎽⎺

You can set subscript and superscript x_y x^y as well, and also make a section of text all caps K :

was an hour late. Buda-
Pesth seeMS A WONDerful
place, from the glimpse

Or small caps K :

ice, from the glimpse
iich I GOT OF IT From t

As well as various other emphasis options such as strike through ℯ, and outline ℚ. When you start with the outline option the outline is the same colour as the basic text. So it looks like BOLD:

Munich at 8:35 P.M.
st May, arriving at
Vienna early next

You can change the outline colour of the text using the line colour option:

Black   ▼   ██   100 %

You can also change the size of the outline from the

Line

tab in the same way that you can with any other outline. For example setting

Line Width: 18.00 pt   ▲▼

with the colours:

And a larger font size will result in something like:

Munich at 8:35 P.M., on
1st May, arriving at
Vienna early next

If you then add shadowed text to make the text stand out it can look quite appealing:

Munich at 8:35 P.M., on
1st May, arriving at
Vienna early next

You can also reverse the text Я .

Style Settings

We've already dealt with how to apply styles at an individual paragraph level using the story editor. But you can click onto the Style Settings in the text properties to change the style of an entire text frame at a time. Click onto the box under Paragraph Style to get a list of all the styles in your document and choose the appropriate one for the text frame.

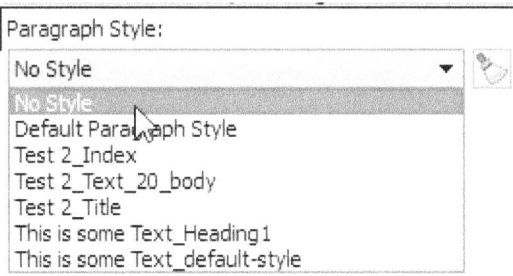

If you select a portion of text you can also apply a paragraph style directly to that portion.

You can also set character styles using this tab.

First Line Offset

The first line offset is the distance from the top of the first line of text to the frame. You can set it using the First Line Offset tab. By default it's set to Maximum Ascent, i.e. to be as close to the top of the frame as possible, but you can also set it to use the font ascent, or the same distance as your line spacing.

Personally I prefer the default option but it might be worth experimenting to see if you like the other options.

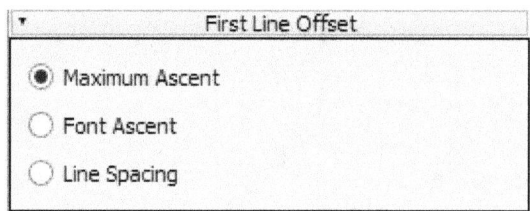

Columns & Text Distances

We've already seen most of these options. Click on 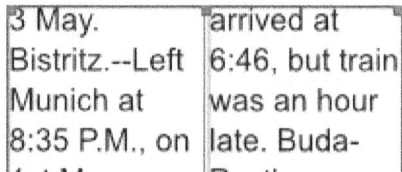 to set the number of columns in a text frame, the gap between the columns:

Produces a small gap between each column:

```
3 May.         arrived at
Bistritz.--Left 6:46, but train
Munich at      was an hour
8:35 P.M., on  late. Buda-
```

And also the ability to set any gap that you want above, below, or to the left or right of the columns:

Top:	0.00 pt	
Bottom:	0.00 pt	
Left:	0.00 pt	
Right:	0.00 pt	

Tabulators control the distance that is travelled when you press the tab key or indent the text. First select all the text that you want to indent. In theory you could just select the text frame but I find that this simply doesn't work as well as selecting the text.

Then, to set the tabulators make sure you are in the column and Text Distances settings and then click:

Tabulators...

Move the mouse to the position on the ruler where you want the first tab:

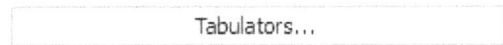

When you click, you'll see the new tab added to the ruler:

You can click and hold on the tab and then move it left or right to shift it to a different position. When you do this all the text that you've indented 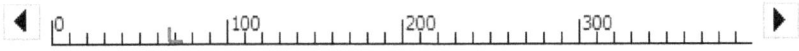 should shift to match the new settings.

You can delete the tabs that you've set by clicking on Delete All . When you're happy with the settings that you've chosen click OK to close the dialogue and apply the settings to the text that you have selected.

Optical Margins

You can use Optical Margins to control the white space around text when you're using justification automatically. Click on

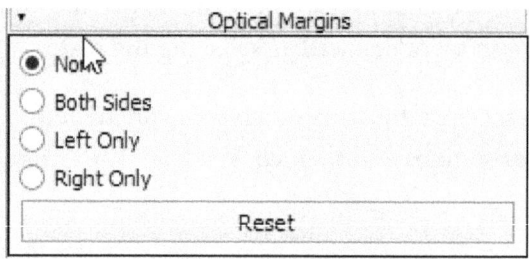

and you'll be able to set the margin so that it's either both sides, left or right only.

If you set these options Scribus will do its best to use hyphenation and differing gaps between words in order to make the result an aesthetically pleasing empty margin around the text.

Sometimes you may have to use the hyphenation options above to manipulate this a little bit. For example it can be necessary to use non breaking spaces with certain words unless you want them broken up onto multiple lines.

Advanced Settings

The advanced settings allow you extra control over the size of the text. They're not things most users will need to consider but if you're (for example) trying to reduce the number of printed pages in a book by ten or fifteen percent to save money without compromising the appearance of the book they can be very useful.

You can set the offset to base ↕T 0.00 % ⬍ the distance between letters in a word A|V 0.00 % ⬍ and scale character widths and heights T 100.00 % ⬍ IT 100.00 % ⬍ .

These options can make a lot of difference in the length of a document. For example, adding an extra point to the distance between letters in a word could add twenty pages to a paperback book. Each of these changes add up.

The Word tracking option is used with justification to try to make sure that you don't get those awkward lines with huge amounts of white space

Word Tracking
Min: 100.00 % ⬍ Norm: 100.00 % ⬍

A similar option is the Glyph Extension which allows you to shrink or increase the space assigned to particular characters slightly to make sure that the words fit properly.

Glyph Extension
Min: 100.00 % ⬍ Max: 100.00 % ⬍

I suggest that with both of these options you don't use too wide a gap between the minimum and the norm or the min and the max values. I find that if the gap is too large the page can start to look a bit strange.

Document Typeset Properties

Setting typesetting properties at the frame level can give you advanced control over the appearance of the document but it is often good to make sure that you set many properties correctly at the document level. If you make too many changes at the Frame level the appearance of the document can be subtly incoherent (to use an artistic term you break the unity of the design and the document that you are working on looks disjointed).

You can use 🔳 Document Setup... in the File Menu to set many of the options for your document as a whole. Where you change Text Frame settings individually those will take precedence over the document settings. I'd suggest being careful when you change individual settings that you don't deviate too far from the master settings.

The Document Settings window looks pretty complicated at first. It's separated into categories that are in icon based tabs on the left hand of the screen, and the actual settings on the right hand.

When I say something like "Click on Document Information" in the Category tab, I'm referring to the tab on the left hand of the screen:

You may often have to scroll down to find the category that I'm asking you to click on.

Setting the Baseline Grid

So far in this tutorial we've discussed aligning text to the baseline grid but we didn't talk about how to change the baseline grid. You

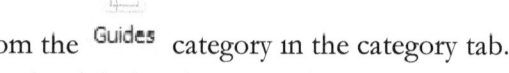

can set the baseline grid from the Guides category in the category tab. Click on it, and then look at the right hand corner of the screen.

Baseline Settings

| Baseline Grid: | 14.40 pt |
| Baseline Offset: | 0.00 pt |

Baseline Grid determines how wide each grid is, and Baseline Offset is the distance from the top of the frame to the beginning of the baseline.

Setting Typography Options

To set typography options click on Typography in the category list.

Most of these options are pretty obvious. For example, subscript and superscript scaling is how small the characters are compared to the basic font size, and displacement is how far above or below the base line the subscript or superscript characters will me.

The underline and strikeout options allow you to control the line width, and also the line width. While it's possible to set these options I personally leave the automatic setting intact since I find that it produces very nice results.

With Small Caps the scaling is compared to a normal capital letter. Automatic Line Spacing will add a little bit of extra space when a line contains small caps letters.

It can be worth experimenting with these settings. Although I find that the default options are actually very good, and I find that if scaling is too low you get the odd situation that the capital letters are smaller than the normal letters. So I recommend that if you change the scaling option you only increase it rather than reduce it.

Small Caps		Automatic Line Spacing	
Scaling:	75 % ⬍	Line Spacing:	20 % ⬍

Some of these settings are matters of taste and opinion, and since everyone has their own taste it can be worth experimenting to see if you can do better than the default options. However, I also recommend saving the document FIRST before you alter any of these settings. That way if you don't like the changes you can always back out of them.

When applying settings I find that sometimes it's better to save your document and then start Scribus again because sometimes it seems like changes don't take until the next time that Scribus loads up.

15 WORKING WITH SCRIBUS

So far we've done a lot of work with different types of frames. Most of the work has been with text and images because that's what we use most when we're laying out a document. In this tutorial I'm going to describe some of the miscellaneous features that can be useful when you're working in a document.

Preview

Scribus has a lot of things like Guides, Frame Edges and so on that won't actually be displayed in the final document. You can turn off all of these things by running a preview. Click on

 in the View window.

For example, if we have the following document:

This is a title

This is some .... random text. there's going t

Running a preview makes it look like:

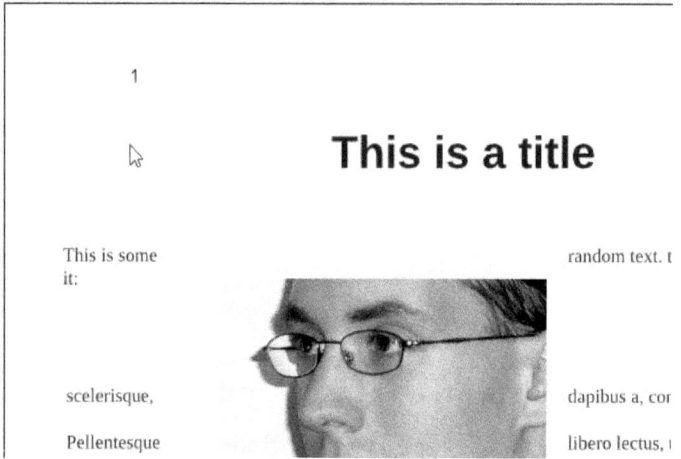

Or, in other words, Preview mode shows you what is on the document.

View

The View Menu offers you a lot of control over how much the document you're working on is shrunk or expanded. When you change these options you're not changing anything fundamental in the document. You're not actually making the document any larger or smaller when you print it out, for example, you're just changing how Scribus displays the document.

The first options will shrink the document either to fit by height or by width of the document. These options are useful when you want to see the entire document on the screen at once.

You can also choose a zoom level. I.e. if you want the page to take up half the size on screen that it does in reality you'd choose 50%. The 100% option is interesting because it'll take up one centimetre of screen space for each centimetre of document.

Why wouldn't you choose to use 100% all the time? Well, the higher zoom sizes are useful if you want to focus on the details of a particular image or part of the document. The smaller zooms allow you to see the entire layout of the document at any one time.

If you're like me you'll find that you switch between different zoom levels depending on the task.

Measurements

Sometimes, you may want to measure the distance between two points in the document. To do this click on

in the Windows menu. You'll see the mouse change to when you move it onto the document. Click where you want to begin measuring, and then move to the point in the document that you want to end measuring.

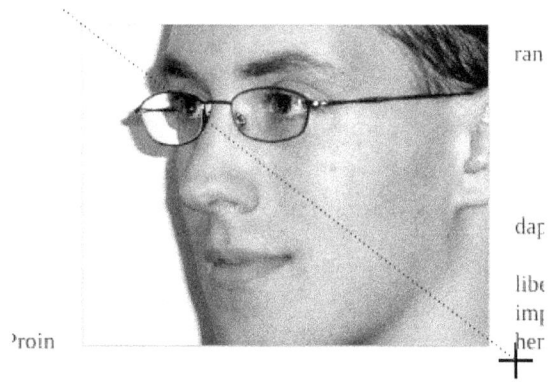

sse platea dictumst. Suspendisse potenti. Vivamus vitae n

You'll see the Distances dialogue. This will show you the X and Y position of the first measurement (X1, Y1) and the end measurement (X2,Y2) as well as the length and the angle.

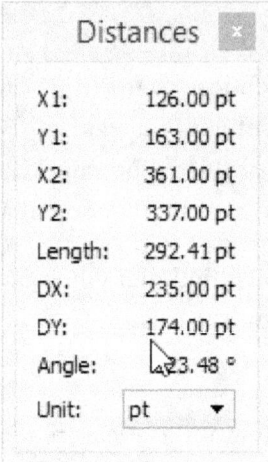

You can change the Unit to something like inches (in) or centimetres (cm) which makes more sense to you if you want to.

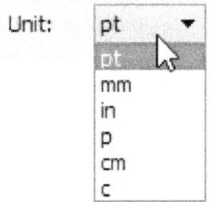

Barcode

While this seems like an odd thing for Scribus to support the reality is that many magazine and other product suppliers will want to add a barcode to their document. You can do this by clicking on

 in the Insert menu.

The first thing to do is choose the type of barcode.

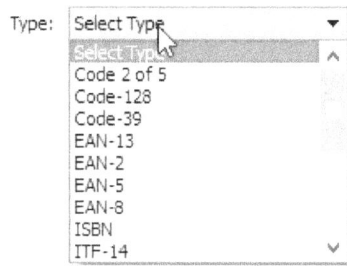

Then enter the barcode itself:

Code: 05443464

Choose whether to toggle on (by clicking the square show it shows a tick) the ☑ Include Text in Barcode option or the ☐ Guard Whitespace option. Most barcodes will require a checksum (which is a way of making sure that the barcode doesn't contain any errors) so you'll probably generally toggle on ☑ Include Checksum Digit .

Once you've chosen all your options, including setting the colours if necessary (although I think the default colours are the best ones for most systems) click OK Your mouse will change to the insert barcode pointer and clicking anywhere on the document will insert the barcode at that point.

Note that you can set the properties for how text flows around a barcode in the same way that you can for an image, by right clicking and then selecting Properties F2 then Group .

Action History

Action History allows you to view a list of the things that you've done to the document. You can turn it on by clicking on

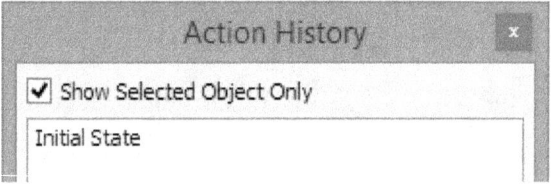 in the Edit menu (click on it a second time to turn it off).

When you click on 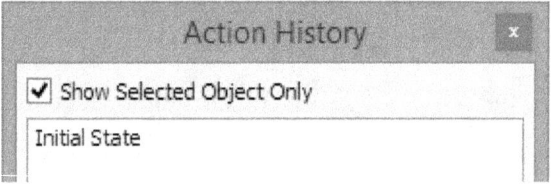 in the view menu the initial information won't be very edifying:

I find that it's important to click the 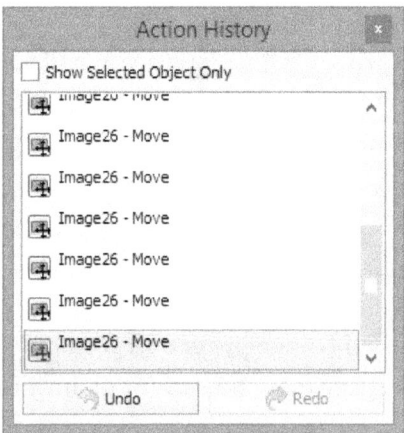 to get the most information from the window that you can. You'll see a list of actions that you've made.

Each item on the list belongs to one action. If you click on it, it will undo everything up to that point. You'll see that the items that you have undone all go into italic.

Click on an italic item and all the actions up to and including that point in the history list are redone.

If you've undone an action (i.e. it is in italics) and then do something like edit, insert, or resize / move a frame all the items that you have undone are permanently lost. So be careful.

The Scrapbook

In the same way that you can use the scratch area to temporarily remove an object from the page that you're editing you can also use the scrapbook. This is a way of handling all sorts of objects that you may need at some later date. You can click on Scrapbook in the windows menu to show the Scrapbook Window:

Right Click on an object and select Send to Scrapbook > Main

You will see an option to give the entry a name:

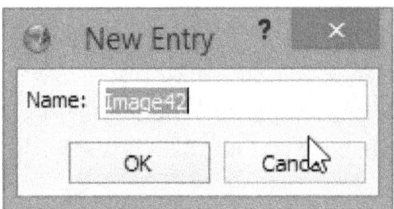

Type in the name and press enter. You'll now see the object added to the scrapbook.

Double clicking on an object will add it to the current page. With most objects this works smoothly. With some image object I find that it doesn't work so well. For some reason you end up with a frame of the correct shape and properties which has lost the image.

However, it does tell you the name of the original image so it's pretty easy to add it back to the frame.

You can save the scrapbook by clicking on and using the save as dialogue. Or load the scrapbook by clicking on . It's even possible to add a new scrapbook page by clicking on and creating or choosing a new directory although I don't often find it necessary to go to those lengths.

Layers

We've already discussed Levels within a layer. These levels determine what objects in a layer hide other objects. For example, you can increase the level of an object by using the outline window or by right clicking on the object and hovering your mouse over Level.

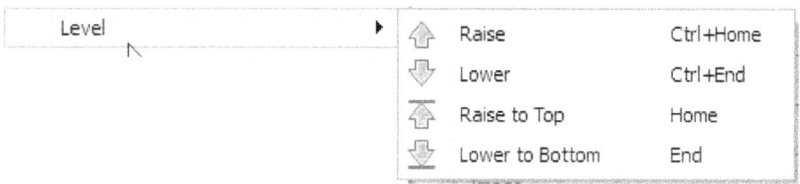

Layers are fundamentally similar to levels. In fact, in the default scenario where you just have a background layer and Levels are the dominant way to control what's object is on top where there are two objects that "should" cover the same space.

But adding Layers into the mix complicates this scenario. An object on the same Layer as another object can be raised or lowered as normal. But if an object is on a Higher or Lower layer than the objects, all objects on the Higher layer will go on top of all objects on the lower layer.

It's also possible to hide all the objects in a layer, i.e. make them all invisible.

Click on Layers F6 in the Windows menu to show the Layers window.

By default there is just one Layer, the Background Layer.

Click on 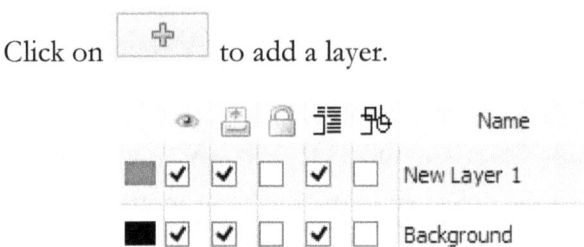 to add a layer.

The New Layer is on top of the background layer. Note that it is highlighted. The layer that you're currently editing is highlighted in the Layers window. If you add a new frame you'll see that the object goes on top of the object in lower layers.

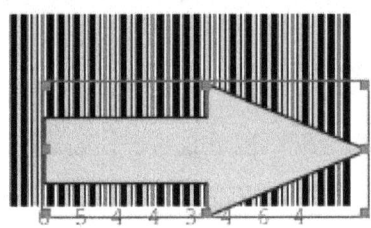

There is a column of toggle boxes under the . This is the visible column. If you toggle the visibility of a layer off:

You'll see that the object goes invisible:

Note that there are several other columns. The toggle boxes under determine if a layer can be printed. This is useful when a document can be displayed on a screen and then printed out. Objects that can't be printed out can be kept in a separate layer.

The column under deals with locking a layer so you can't edit the objects on the layer. This can be useful when you've got objects in a layer that you don't want to accidentally alter while you're editing objects in another layer. Makes text frames in lower levels flow around objects that are in higher levels.

Double click on the name of a layer to change it.

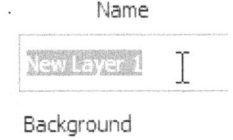

You can raise the level of a layer by clicking on its name to select it:

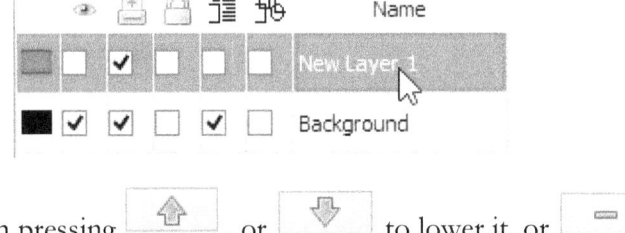

And then pressing , or to lower it, or

to remove the layer altogether. If you remove a layer you'll be asked if you want to remove all the objects on it. If you choose yes they'll obviously be deleted.

If you choose to keep the objects they'll be added to the layer beneath the one that you're deleting.

If you select a layer you can choose how much it obscures the layers beneath it ^{Opacity:} 100 % and you can even choose how Scribus will blend layers together. I.e. the default option of hiding the object that's on the lower layer isn't the only choice. You can also choose whether to use other options such as darkening, lightening etc.

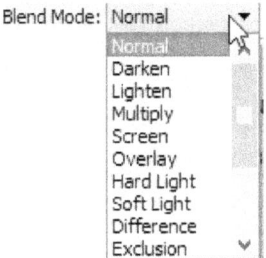

As a general rule I don't use these Blend Modes much, although it can be worth experimenting to see the effect on your document if you have a special requirement.

Moving an object between layers.
Right click on the object and hover your mouse over Send to Layer. Then select the layer that you want to move the object to.

Saving a File as a Template

We've already discussed the ability to create a file from a

template. A template is a combination of settings, frames, masterpages, images and text that you can use to create a new document. In other words, Scribus copies all the setting and design work you've already done and then lets you modify it and add to it.

To save your current file as a template click on

Save as Template...   Ctrl+Alt+S in the File menu. You'll see a

Save As dialogue. I recommend leaving the directory setting at the default in this case, and just choosing the name of the template. If you've done work on the colour profiles or fonts I think you should toggle these options on.

☐ Include Fonts   ☐ Include Colour Profiles

When you next come to create a new file from template, the document you've just saved will be one of the options.

I recommend taking care when you make a template because it may be in use for a long time so extra design work often pays dividends.

16 EXPORTING YOUR DOCUMENT

Before exporting a file I recommend running the Preflight Verifier. It makes sure that you haven't got any errors in the document which means that you won't have problems during the export.

It can also be necessary to install GhostScript (see above) if you want to export or check some formats.

Exporting Text from a Frame

To export Text from a Frame right click on the Frame and then Hover your mouse over Export and click on

| Save Text... |

. This will bring up a save as dialogue. Choose the file name and directory and click ok.

Exporting EPS or SVG

Both EPS (Post Script) and SVG (a form of image file) are used by various printing companies when you print an offset or print on demand magazine or book. You can choose either option by hovering your mouse over Export in the File menu and then clicking on the appropriate section.

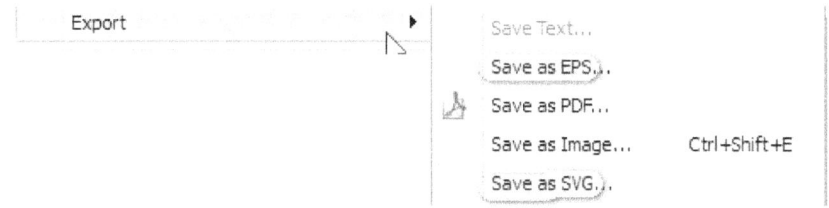

In both of these cases you just get a save as dialogue where you choose the directory and then the file name of the file to be saved.

It's important that when you are exporting an EPS file that you have GhostScript installed otherwise the option won't work.

Exporting PDF

The export to PDF option can be selected by hovering your mouse over Export in the File menu and clicking on Save as PDF.

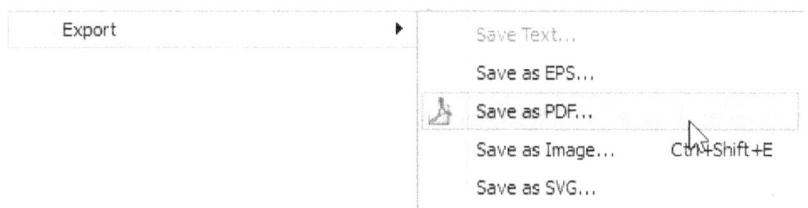

You must have GhostScript installed before you try to export to pdf. Also, it's generally best to make sure that you have run a preflight verifier.

The dialogue for exporting to PDF is complicated. The first section is, however, pretty obvious. It shows you the output file location:

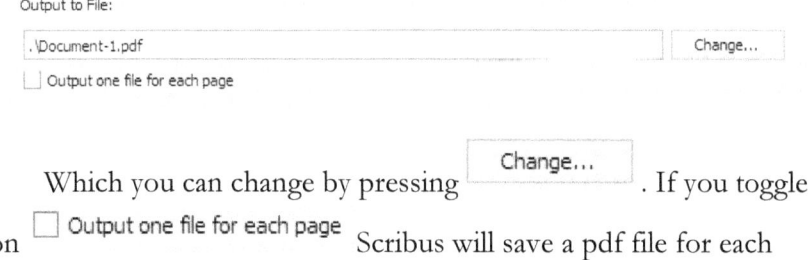

Which you can change by pressing Change... . If you toggle on Output one file for each page Scribus will save a pdf file for each page. That can be a heck of a lot of files sometimes, so I don't recommend that you use this option unless you've made sure you're saving the files to a new, empty directory.

It's the rest of the dialogue that is pretty complicated. You've got a tab bar with common options:

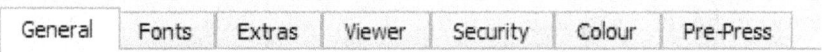

One thing to realise is that you often won't need to change some of these options. For example, if you're just printing out the document on your own printer you won't need to change the Font options.

General PDF Options

Selecting Printing Pages

The first section of options allows you to print

to ⦿ All Pages   or selected pages   ○ Choose Pages   . Click on the round button to choose between these options. If you choose selected pages you can specify a group of comma separated range of pages like you would when you are printing out a document. For example the following document exports pages 1, 3, 4:

⦿ Choose Pages

| 1,3-4 | ••• |

You can also choose to rotate the pages if you like.

☐ Clip to Printer Margins   is a special option that makes sure that you remove anything that isn't within the printer margins. If you don't toggle this option on Scribus will scale the page so that everything in your document is included in the export.

Compressing Text and Vector Graphics

Scribus offers you the option to choose whether to compress the document or not. Compressing a document can be a good idea – but only if you don't intend to print it out in a commercial printer. Otherwise it's possible that you will lose some of the granularity in images.

Most commercial printers will print out at 300 dpi, and compressing images further than that can cause quite a few problems.

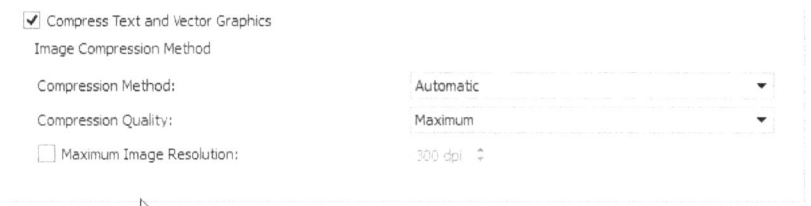

So these options are best used when you're creating a print out at home, or when you're creating a document that is meant for display on a computer screen.

You can choose the compression method and quality, and you can also set the maximum resolution of images in your document by toggling on the field:

And then entering the correct resolution in the field 300 dpi . Note that if you set this option much higher than the maximum resolution of the printer or screen you'll use to display the document you will be using a lot of space that you don't need to use.

File Options
The first option allows you to set what version of the PDF

format your file should comply with. It's a crucial choice in some circumstances since different printers can require different formats. Also, some features that are available in later formats aren't available in the earlier formats.

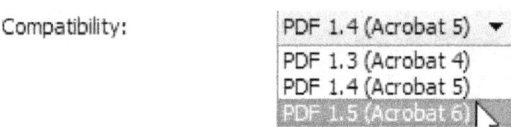

If you run the preflight verifier with your choice of versions of PDF you'll be reasonably sure that the export will work.

As a general rule you won't change the binding unless you're using a language other than English. The option is there for the rare occasion you need it, though. Binding is literally the place you'd put the staple or binding on after you print out the document.

Binding: Left Margin   ▼

Why's it important? Because Scribus gives you a little extra space on the binding side of the document to account for the binding when you print it out.

Most of the other file options are pretty obvious, but one that might be important is ☐ Include Layers . If you choose to include layers the file won't be "flattened" and will be rejected by a lot of printing companies as an error. Similarly, sometimes Scribus decides to export Shapes and Text Frames as Graphics, and if you choose to reduce the resolution for these objects below 300 you'll find that many printers complain Resolution for EPS Graphics: 300 dpi .

Font Options

Click on Fonts in the PDF options tab to choose your Font options.

The Font Options allow you to choose which Fonts to embed.

The embedding process results in a larger file, but if you don't Embed your fonts you run the risk that your version of, say, Calibri will be slightly different than the printers. So your document will look different.

As a rule, Scribus will try to embed all the Fonts in your document:

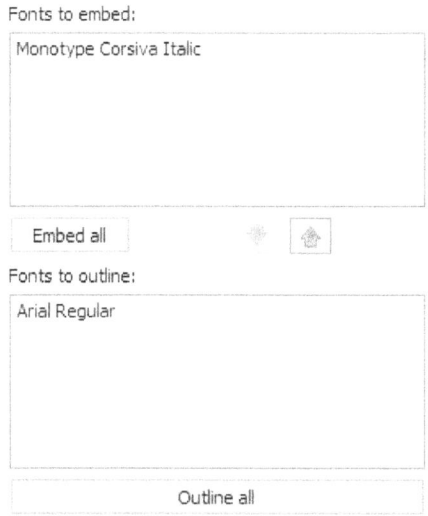

But it won't always succeed. Some Fonts won't allow themselves to be embedded. This is often because many fonts in your computer are copyright to someone else, and the license they have given you to use the font is restricted.

In this case, Scribus will "Outline" the font. This means that the text will be converted to an image. The disadvantage of this is that the file will be very large.

When you see that a font is outlined it is worth checking that you have commercial permission to use it in your document. You don't want to break copyright accidentally!

If you have a very large document try pressing Embed all to

see if any of the fonts that you are using can be embedded, or alternatively substitute similar fonts that can be embedded for fonts that can't be distributed legally.

Extra Options

You can see miscellaneous options by clicking on Extras . These options are basically for Presentations which is a use that I haven't described in this book. Personally, I think that using software like LibreOffice Impress is better for presentations. Which is why I wrote a book on how to use LibreOffice Impress.

Viewer Options

When you look at a PDF file on a computer you're using a PDF viewer. You can use the options in the Viewer tab to control how the document looks. When setting these options it's important to remember that the recipient of the document can override many of them. So there's no guarantee that if you change these options it will have an effect on the final user.

The first set of options is a choice between different viewing modes. For example, single page, continuous or double pages:

Document Layout

◉ Single Page

◯ Continuous

◯ Double Page Left

◯ Double Page Right

The second set of options control how the viewer will act when the document is displayed. For example, if the viewer is in full screen mode, or if you want to hide the toolbar. I personally always leave this at the default setting ◉ Use Viewers Defaults . This is because I think the end user probably knows better how they want to document to appear than you do!

Security Options

Documents can be encrypted so that people can only access it with a password.

Toggle ☐ Use Encryption to turn on the encryptions. Then enter the password. The Owner is the person that can change the document, the User is anyone who wants to view the document.

Owner:

User:

Once you set these passwords the rest is pretty straightforward. If you are the Owner you can set them to prevent people doing things like Printing the document and so on:

Settings

✔ Allow Printing the Document

✔ Allow Changing the Document

✔ Allow Copying Text and Graphics

✔ Allow Adding Annotations and Fields

I think these options are not hugely secure; once someone has the password it would be possible for a dedicated hacker to break through these extra settings. But the existence of encryption and a password at least somewhat reduces the ease of accessing a document. At least for a casual user.

Colour Options

You can set colour options from the Colour tab. The default option is for the screen. You can also choose to create a black and white file (Greyscale) or a file for the Printer.

Output Intended For:	Screen / Web ▾
	Screen / Web
	Printer
	Greyscale

If you choose Printer, you can convert spot colours to process Colours by toggling on ☐ Convert Spot Colours to Process Colours which I'd normally recommend. This will slightly improve the colour of the document because you'll be accounting for the fact that printed documents use a different colour process than screen documents.

You can also choose to manually alter the rendering settings by toggling on ☐ Use Custom Rendering Settings which I don't recommend unless you are an advanced user.

Pre-Press Options

You can control Pre-Press settings from the Pre-Press tab although many of these settings are quite advanced. One particular feature that is often very important is the Bleed setting which allows you to adjust the printed area to take into account cropping. You can also control the output profile which would ordinarily happen only if you had specific instructions from a printer.

The Pre-Press options can display special printing marks such as crop marks that can sometimes be useful if you are an experienced user of DTP software, and can also be used to control the offset of the exported document.

When you're finished setting the options press Save .

Save as Image

Hover your mouse over Export in the File menu and click on Save as Image...   Ctrl+Shift+E .

The first thing you'll see is the option to control which directory to export the images to:

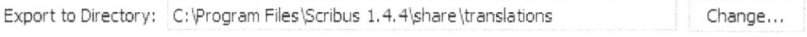

I recommend using a directory that is empty (i.e. one you create). In any case, click  to browse for the directory you want to save the images to.

The next choice is the Range of pages to Export. This works the same way as a Print Dialogue or the previous export to PDF dialogue. You can choose to export the current page, all pages, or a comma separated range.

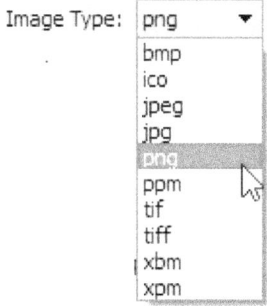

Finally, you can choose the settings for the images that you're going to Export. The first choice is the format of the image.

Then next choice is the quality and resolution of the image. A normal screen is at 72 dpi, and most printers will print out at 300 dpi for the best quality.

Quality: Automatic

Resolution: 72 dpi

Size: 100 %

You can use   to scale the image so that it's smaller than the normal page size. When you're happy click on   OK   .

17 OBJECTS

Align and Distribute

Most of the time I move objects around the screen freely, or I snap them to grid, but there is the functionality in Scribus to align (i.e. to put the work either on the left, centre, or right hand side) or distribute (move objects together so they match a particular distribution pattern) objects automatically. This can be useful when you want to make sure that the document is visually balanced and appealing.

Align

First select the object (or, if you want to align more than one object at a time select both objects by clicking on the first then holding the shift key down as you click on the other objects to align) that you want to move and then click on

Align and Distribute   in the windows menu.

You need to decide what you're going to align relative to. Some of these options are obvious, such as aligning it to the page or the margins within the page. First selected is the first object that is in the selection, and last selected is the last object in the selection.

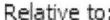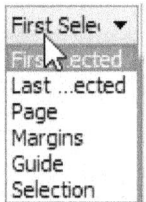

You can then select a guide (if that's what you're aligning relative to) and how you want to align the object. I generally find that aligning by resizing often doesn't look as good as aligning by moving the object.

Finally, click on the icon that graphically matches the alignment that you want.

For example, aligns one object below the other object:

Like normal you can get a description of each icon by hovering your mouse over it, although the pictures do a pretty good job of explaining what an icon will do:

Distribute

In the Align and Distribute window that we opened in the last step click on the Distribute tab.

While distributing the distance is generally automatic. But if you set Distance: 0.00 p then you can force the vertical gap between the objects to the size you've chosen.

Once you've chosen the distance you can choose the Distribution option.

For example,  makes the horizontal gap between the edges and the side of the page equal:

Again, you can hover your mouse over one of the icons to read a description of what it does.

Grouping objects together

You often want to treat several objects as if they were the same object. For example, say you want to caption an image:

This is the picture of a man

What you don't want is to have to move the caption separately from the image. Both items are intellectually related, so you want to be able to move, resize, cut or treat them like the same object.

A group of objects is just such a relationship: one which Scribus almost treats as if it is a single object. We've already seen a group in the Barcode section. We can move a barcode or resize it even though it's actually made up of a lot of separate shapes.

To make a group you've got to select all the objects. First, click on the first object, then hold the shift key down and select the next object, keeping the shift held down until you've selected all the objects that you want:

Right click on one of the objects and click

Group	Ctrl+G

.

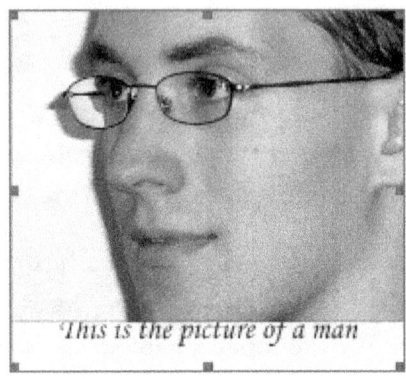

This is the picture of a man

You'll notice that when you select one object, move it or resize it you'll do it to both objects. At least until you right click on the group and select Ungroup   Ctrl+Shift+G .

Controlling the Opacity of a group

We've already seen how objects by default hide other objects beneath them. For example:

This   will hide

This is the picture of a man

You can change this behaviour by clicking on

Properties   F2   and then

 and adjusting the opacity down Opacity: 100 .

For example Opacity: 30 produces an image like:

Locking an Object

When you lock an object you prevent anyone from moving the object by accident. Right click on the object that you want to lock and click Is Locked   Ctrl+L . When you try to select it you'll see that the rectangles you use to resize it have gone, and if you try to move it or change it you won't be able to (although you can still change some of the object properties using the properties window):

Right click on an object that you've locked and then click on  again in order to unlock it.

Preventing an image being resizable

Sometimes you may wish to move and change an object but still prevent resizing. To do this right click on the object and select . To unlock the size right click on the object and then on .

Controlling Colours

In the same way that a document has a default style scheme which you can edit, a document also has a colour scheme. There are standard colours that you can choose from as well as adding new colours using the colour wheel. I've already shown you how to do this.

It's possible to control this colour palette through the colour editor. This allows you to add, delete, and even import a colour scheme.

Click on   Colours...   in the edit menu.

You'll see a list of colours in the left of the screen.

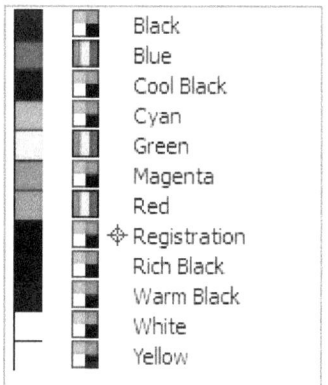

If you hover your mouse over one of the colours you'll see a tool tip that tells you what combination of red green and blue it is.

Click on a colour once and you'll see that you can delete the colour by clicking on Delete and you can also copy it by clicking on Duplicate . This is useful where you might want the same colour but a lighter or darker shade.

You can create a new colour by clicking on New or change an existing colour by clicking on Edit . These options will bring up an Edit colour dialogue.

The first step is to make sure that you change the name to something sensible:

If you're an expert user you could change the colour mapping method:

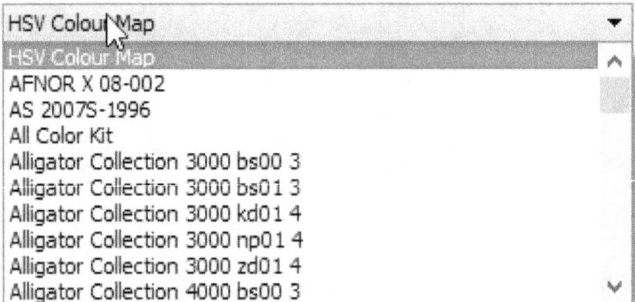

But honestly the way I mostly use this window is to select the colour closest to the one I want on the colour map by clicking on it and then moving the mouse pointer while I've got the button held down:

All the while watching the preview box at the bottom. You can then make fine adjustment to individual parts of the colour (i.e. Cyan, Magenta etc.) by using the slide bar:

If you're happy click [OK] .

Note that the final option is to remove all unused colours in the palette by clicking on [Remove Unused] . Click [OK] when you're happy with the changes that you have made to the colours. Remember that these changes can be hard to undo sometimes so be careful that you don't make any changes that you will regret.

Replacing Colours

This is a slightly dangerous option because you're making wholesale changes to a document. Before you try using it I'd make sure to save the document. But sometimes you may want to replace all the instances of one colour in a document with another colour.

Click on  in the edit menu.

Initially you'll see an empty list:

Click on 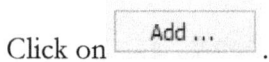 .

Choose the colour you want to replace:

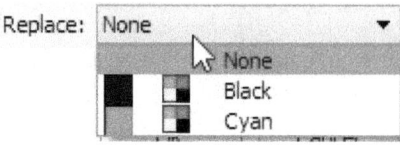

And the colour you want to replace it with:

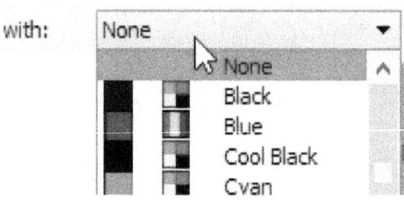

Then click on 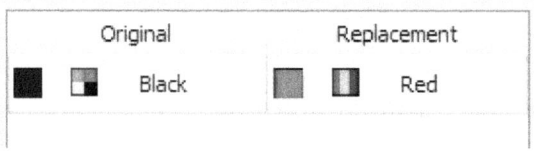 . You'll see the replacement added to the list.

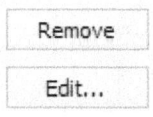

You can click on a replacement on the list to remove it or edit it.

Until you press 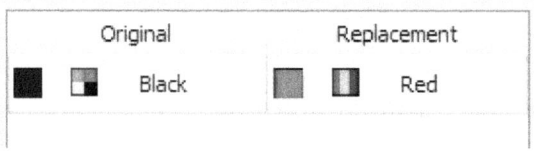 in the replace colour dialogue nothing will happen to the document but when you click

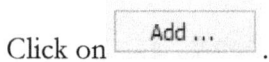 all the instances of the original colour will be replaced. So you can make a huge number of changes to the document in one go.

Manage Images

When you're working on a large document it can be useful to be able to find a particular image. Click on  in the extras menu to bring up the manage images dialogue. This consists of a list of images that you have in the document:

You can right click on the image pane to choose how to sort the list 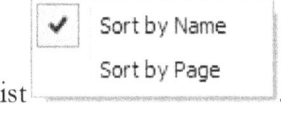.

When you click on one of the images you get its location and name as well as the effective DPI of the image:

On Page: 1
Page Item: Image2
Effective DPI: 256 x 256

Click on Go to to go to the page of the image or Select to go to the correct page and then select the image. If you want to find the location of the image on the disk click Search....

Thanks and So Long

Thank you for getting to this point in the book! I hope you've enjoyed using Scribus as much as I've enjoyed writing this book. I think the ability to do all your document layout using a free piece of software – compared to, say, Adobe's CC which can cost a lot of money – is pretty cool.

At this point in the book you probably know enough to create your own book!

If you've got any questions or comments don't hesitate to contact me. My email address is thomasecclestone@yahoo.co.uk . I've enjoyed writing this book. I hope you've enjoyed using it, and I wish you good luck.

ABOUT THE AUTHOR

Thomas Ecclestone is a software engineer and technical writer who lives in Kent, England. After getting his 1st class honours in software engineering he worked at the National Computing Centre in Manchester, the Manchester Metropolitan University, and for BEC systems Integration before starting his own business in software development. He is a writer who lives on a smallholding in Kent where he looks after a small flock of Hebridean sheep.